Informal Meditations for Informal People

Informal Meditations for Informal People

The Sunday Gospel for the Rest of the Week
(Cycle C)

Ferruccio Parazzoli

Translated
by
Matthew J. O'Connell

A Liturgical Press Book

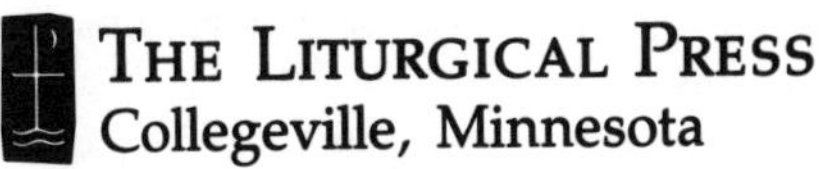

Informal Meditations for Informal People: The Sunday Gospel for the Rest of the Week (Cycle C) was originally published by Edizioni Paoline (Milan, Italy) under the title *Breviario familiare: Il Vangelo della domenica per tutti i giorni della settimana* © 1987 by Figlie di San Paolo.

Bible texts are from the Revised Standard Version.

Cover design by Mary Furth.

1 2 3 4 5 6 7 8 9

Library of Congress Cataloging-in-Publication Data

Parazzoli, Ferruccio, 1935–
[Breviario familiare. English]
Informal meditations for informal people : the Sunday Gospel for the rest of the week, cycle C / Ferruccio Parazzoli ; translated by Matthew J. O'Connell.
p. cm.
Translation of: Breviario familiare.
ISBN 0-8146-1843-X
1. Church year meditations. 2. Bible. N.T. Gospels—Meditations. 3. Devotional calendars—Catholic Church. 4. Catholic Church—Prayer-books and devotions—English. I. Title.
BX2170.C55P32 1991 90-36015
242'.3—dc20 CIP

Contents

Sundays and Feasts

Preface

A commentary on the Gospel is always, to some extent, a commentary on one's own life. When one carries on this kind of reflection for a whole year, as I have done once each week in the pages of *Famiglia Cristiana,* one is certain to become aware of one's own inadequacy. The inadequacy I have in mind is not an inadequacy in commenting on the Gospel texts; after all, all of us are inadequate in this respect. I am referring rather to an inadequacy of life. I have become aware, week after week, that our life is reduced to a trite stammering, a confused mumbling caught between yes and no. We are unable to determine just what place awaits us in the bedlam of daily life or even whether there is a place for us all. We are disoriented and therefore often deeply saddened.

The weekly reading of the Gospel and the task of commenting on it as a layman, an ordinary fellow, have convinced me that there is indeed a way of living our human life. But it is a scandalous way and one that is perhaps quite displeasing to the cunning hidden persuader—be he named Satan, Belial, or Beelzebub—in whom I continue to believe. The way I mean is the way of laughter. I am convinced that Christians must learn to laugh or lose the battle in which they are engaged. They must learn to express their scorn publicly for the grotesque triumphal procession of sad gods: money, power, success, beauty, sex, excitement, and even good health. In short, they must learn to laugh at all the wretched forms of enslavement that are daily merchandised as promising happiness. They must acquire once again the ability to say no. The Gospel teaches us that the emperor, whoever he be, is always naked. Well then, why not laugh at him? Laughter is more scandalous than tears; it is also more difficult to laugh than to weep. Especially to laugh at the fetishes that have enslaved us, beginning with the fetish we have made of ourselves.

These brief pages are therefore offered as a kind of breviary for the ordinary person, the "one without qualities," the only one who can still be saved in a world in which everyone boasts, like a salesman in the marketplace, of his or her own marvelous and unparalleled perfections. Am I asking, then, for a rediscovery of the humble? Yes, but even more a rediscovery of Christian courage. My wish is that reflection on the Gospel will lead us to the discovery that if we are oppressed, it is solely because we have sold everything, even our souls. We are afraid of life only because we are constantly making the same mistake: the mistake of not believing in Christ's every word and in every letter of every word.

Ferruccio Parazzolli

Rejoice in the Lord always;
again I will say, Rejoice.
The Lord is at hand.
(Phil 4:4-5)

Expectation and Coming of the Lord

The Courage of Children

(First Sunday of Advent)

There will be signs in sun and moon and stars, and upon the earth distress of nations in perplexity at the roaring of the sea and the waves, men fainting with fear and with foreboding of what is coming on the world; for the powers of the heavens will be shaken.

And then they will see the Son of man coming in a cloud with power and great glory.

Now when these things begin to take place, look up and raise your heads, because your redemption is drawing near.

But take heed to yourselves lest your hearts be weighed down with dissipation and drunkenness and cares of this life, and that day come upon you suddenly like a snare; for it will come upon all who dwell upon the face of the whole earth. But watch at all times, praying that you may have strength to escape all these things that will take place, and to stand before the Son of man.

(Luke 21:25-28, 34-36)

***

Look—we tell our children—today we begin waiting for Christmas. And we see them smiling. For a moment remembrance of the past and expectation of the future overlap in our minds. Time in its daily course seems to follow a broader, more restful rhythm, like a deep breath taken after tension that has lasted too long.

Expectation is something restful but also disturbing; it is like a continual tension that is never allowed to let up: In the morning we look forward to the repose of evening and the ritual of meal and family around the table; in the evening we look forward anxiously to the morning, when responsibilities and worries await us. But once we begin expecting Christmas we hear the Gospel telling us: Look around, observe the world, see how disturbed it is, see the agitation that sweeps through it like a wind that never dies down. Look at yourself: Each of us can say in the evening, as we lie in bed ready to put out the light, "Lord, I may not be weighed down with dissipation and drunkenness, but my heart is certainly full of anxieties."

Now we are told that our deliverance is at hand because the Son of Man is coming. But we are not able to "look up and raise our heads," for life still makes us fearful. I once heard a missionary priest say as he was setting out for Peru, "Fear is not a Christian feeling." Since then I have repeated this sentence every morning on the elevator as it sweeps me down into the traffic of every day. It is true: What is there to be afraid of if Christ is coming to save us and is already in our midst? We may, therefore, continue to wait: alertly, attentively, and joyously, just like our children. And, after all, who has more courage than a child in facing life? Who waits more hopefully?

When the Angel Speaks to Us

(Feast of the Immaculate Conception)

In the sixth month the angel Gabriel was sent from God to a city of Galilee named Nazareth, to a virgin betrothed to a man whose name was Joseph, of the house of David; and the virgin's name was Mary. And he came to her and said, "Hail, full of grace, the Lord is with you!" But she was greatly troubled at the saying, and considered in her mind what sort of greeting this might be. And the angel said to her, "Do not be afraid, Mary, for you have found favor with God. And behold, you will conceive in your womb and bear a son, and you shall call his name Jesus. He will be great and will be called the Son of the Most High; and the Lord God will give to him the throne of his father David, and he will reign over the house of Jacob for ever; and of his kingdom there will be no end."

And Mary said to the angel, "How can this be, since I have no husband?" And the angel said to her, "The Holy Spirit will come upon you, and the power of the Most High will overshadow you; therefore the child to be born will be called holy, the Son of God. And behold, your kinswoman Elizabeth in her old age has conceived a son; and this is the sixth month with her who was called barren. For with God nothing will be impossible." And Mary said, "Behold, I am the handmaid of the Lord; let it be to me according to your word." And the angel departed from her.

(Luke 1:26-38)

***

So the too-often-used words are true: "God needs human beings." To carry out his plan of salvation, he needs what human creatures say about him. The passage from Luke's Gospel that we read today, the Feast of the Immaculate Conception, is a challenge to our human rationalism; it runs counter to our daily experience. A messenger, a creature of a higher nature, presents himself to an ordinary girl of Galilee and tells her something that is mind boggling, something bordering on the unacceptable. Why accept it, then? Because "nothing is impossible with God." You must take it or leave it, all or nothing.

Mary does not say anything; she is disturbed and speaks only to assert her own chastity: "I have no husband." Having said this, she has no further objection to God's will: "Let it be to me according to your word." Nothing else matters; having asserted her dignity as creature and woman before God himself, Mary asks no further questions; she is at the service of the divine plan.

We modern Christians, whose Christianity is so much a matter of habit, never have the terrible thought that Mary might have refused out of fear or unbelief. So incapable are we of recognizing God's plan even in the most logical events of our life, so blind are we and so mistrusting, that we live on the income produced by the faith of that young Jewish girl. If God really needs human beings, as he needed Mary, and if his angel were to come down to us in the street and whisper in our ear amid the noise of traffic or as we sat at our worktable or washed the dishes after supper, if his angel were thus to come, perhaps we would not recognize him. Prudent folk that we are, easily irritated and concerned above all else with our precious mental health, we might well dismiss the voice of God as a bothersome fantasy.

Life Is Not a Riddle

(Third Sunday of Advent)

The multitudes asked John, "What then shall we do?" And he answered them, "He who has two coats, let him share with him who has none; and he who has food, let him do likewise." Tax collectors also came to be baptized, and said to him, "Teacher, what shall we do?" And he said to them, "Collect no more than is appointed you." Soldiers also asked him, "And we, what shall we do?" And he said to them, "Rob no one by violence or by false accusation, and be content with your wages."

As the people were in expectation, and all men questioned in their hearts concerning John, whether perhaps he were the Christ, John answered them all, "I baptize you with water; but he who is mightier than I is coming, the thong of whose sandals I am not worthy to untie; he will baptize you with the Holy Spirit and with fire. His winnowing fork is in his hand, to clear his threshing floor, and to gather the wheat into his granary, but the chaff he will burn with unquenchable fire."

So, with many other exhortations, he preached the good news to the people.

(Luke 3:10-18)

***

''What shall we do?'' No one reading today's Gospel can possibly avoid this question which is asked, urgently and anxiously, three times in the space of a few lines. It is the eternal question that hammers at the minds and hearts of human beings as soon as they become conscious that life is not an accident or an adventure into the unknown or even a game to be won, but something precious that is moving toward a goal and that, if it is to have value, must find the strength for renewal and risk taking. What then are we to do with our lives?

In the final analysis, one need not be a Christian to ask this question. I would even say that it is not a Christian question at all. The answers the Baptist gives are in fact minimal in content; they apply to everyone and at all times: Let those who have superfluous goods be mindful of those who cannot satisfy their hunger; let those who have authority, either for economic reasons or because they have force at their command, not abuse it in dealing with the helpless.

The answer to the question may seem quite simple, but it is not. Among Leo Tolstoy's most disturbing books there is one titled *What, Then, Are We to Do?* (Lenin has a book with the same title.) Here, after citing the first part of the passage from Luke, the author of *War and Peace* shows the absolute powerlessness of human beings and human justice to eliminate the real causes of wretchedness and suffering. The definitive answer to our questions is in fact given only with the coming of Christ and the ''good news.'' Only then, when we have experienced the baptism in Spirit and fire, will we realize that the question ''What are we to do'' is truly a non-Christian question, an idle question which Christ has answered once and for all.

The Risk of Joy

(Fourth Sunday of Advent)

In those days Mary arose and went with haste into the hill country, to a city of Judah, and she entered the house of Zechariah and greeted Elizabeth. And when Elizabeth heard the greeting of Mary, the babe leapt in her womb; and Elizabeth was filled with the Holy Spirit and she exclaimed with a loud cry, "Blessed are you among women, and blessed is the fruit of your womb! And why is this granted me, that the mother of my Lord should come to me? For behold, when the voice of your greeting came to my ears, the babe in my womb leapt for joy. And blessed is she who believed that there would be a fulfillment of what was spoken to her from the Lord."

And Mary said: "My soul magnifies the Lord, and my spirit rejoices in God my Savior, for he has regarded the low estate of his handmaiden."

(Luke 1:39-48)

***

Two women meet and rejoice together over their coming motherhood. The moving spontaneity of Mary and Elizabeth transforms their expectation into a leap of pure joy toward God.

We know that human expectation, even expectation of so wonderful an event as the birth of a child, is never free of worry and anxiety. The future in any form frightens us. We fear for the continuation of our little habitual ways; we have no assurance that we will know how to handle events. Each new day calls into question again all that we are; every new incident may find us unprepared. We are assiduous, anxious searchers for happiness but are incapable of joy. Joy is an utterly pure movement of the soul ("My soul magnifies the Lord") that never springs from self-centeredness, pride, or the fulfillment of our desires. Kept in turmoil by our self-preoccupation, we are content with mediocre kinds of happiness that are always contaminated by fear.

The joy of Mary and Elizabeth is untouched by any apprehension. These women have complete trust in God's word; they are willing instruments of salvation; they are not concerned with themselves, but in their faith they rejoice in the divine promise. "Blessed is she who believed that there would be a fulfillment of what was spoken to her from the Lord."

The spectacle of their joy is so close to us, so concretized in the child that leaps in its mother's womb, that it reminds us of the special gaze, full of light, of the woman whom we love and who has given us children. The expectation of Christmas or of any birthday calls us not only to trust in God but to trust in ourselves and our ability to take risks, to renew ourselves, to face with joyous courage the life which each new day brings.

In Children the Future of God

(Feast of the Holy Family)

Now the parents of Jesus went to Jerusalem every year at the feast of the Passover. And when he was twelve years old, they went up according to custom; and when the feast was ended, as they were returning, the boy Jesus stayed behind in Jerusalem. His parents did not know it, but supposing him to be in the company they went a day's journey, and they sought him among their kinsfolk and acquaintances; and when they did not find him, they returned to Jerusalem, seeking him. After three days they found him in the temple, sitting among the teachers, listening to them and asking them questions; and all who heard him were amazed at his understanding and his answers. And when they saw him they were astonished; and his mother said to him, "Son, why have you treated us so? Behold, your father and I have been looking for you anxiously." And he said to them, "How is it that you sought me? Did you not know that I must be in my Father's house?" And they did not understand the saying which he spoke to them.

And he went down with them and came to Nazareth, and was obedient to them; and his mother kept all these things in her heart. And Jesus increased in wisdom and in stature, and in favor with God and man.

(Luke 2:42-52)

***

"Son, why have you treated us so?" As we read today's Gospel, this is the sentence that immediately strikes us, because we ourselves have perhaps used the same words more than once and because they express so much of our anxiety and love. Only later, when the first feelings have subsided, can we attend to the other points in the story: the picture of Jesus among the teachers; the picture of Jesus growing in wisdom and grace during the subsequent years, which we call "hidden" because we know almost nothing about him until the beginning of his public life.

The words that burst from Mary's heart touch closely; they burn into us; they are our own words uttered here and now, every day, in our families: "Child, why have you treated us so?" Mary spoke them for all of us. The bond that unites every family, as it did the family at Nazareth, must be one of harmony and love. But we must be able to renounce this very bond, precisely because it is based on love and not selfishness, and to renounce, too, this very human rebuke ("Why have you treated us so?"), and we must seek to understand the reasons that lead us beyond it. Joseph and Mary did not understand immediately. We, too, often do not understand the behavior of our children; in these cases we must suspend judgment ("His mother kept all these things in her heart") and replace judgment with trust and love. Often it is only our own fears that make us anxious, for we want no novelty to trouble our family life. But we must be able to surrender this very serenity if we truly believe and desire that each of our children has a whole life to live, whatever form it may take, not according to our myopic wishes but according to the will of God that often remains hidden from us.

The Lengthy Way of Wisdom

(The Epiphany of the Lord)

Now when Jesus was born in Bethlehem of Judea in the days of Herod the king, behold, wise men from the East came to Jerusalem, saying, "Where is he who has been born king of the Jews? For we have seen his star in the East, and have come to worship him." When Herod the king heard this, he was troubled, and all Jerusalem with him; and assembling all the chief priests and scribes of the people, he inquired of them where the Christ was to be born. They told him, "In Bethlehem of Judea; for so it is written by the prophet:

> *'And you, O Bethlehem, in the land of Judah,*
> *are by no means least among the rulers of Judah;*
> *for from you shall come a ruler*
> *who will govern my people Israel.'"*

Then Herod summoned the wise men secretly and ascertained from them what time the star appeared; and he sent them to Bethlehem, saying, "Go and search diligently for the child, and when you have found him bring me word, that I too may come and worship him."

When they had heard the king they went their way; and lo, the star which they had seen in the East went before them, till it came to rest over the place where the child was. When they saw the star, they rejoiced exceedingly with great joy; and going into the house they saw the child with Mary his mother, and they fell down and worshiped him. Then, opening their treasures, they offered him gifts, gold and frankincense and myrrh. And being warned in a dream not to return to Herod, they departed to their own country by another way.

(Matt 2:1-12)

***

These beloved, mysterious characters, the Magi, delighted us in childhood. They used to arrive, a little out of breath, for the last of the Christmas feasts; in fact, they were taken from their big box only on the eve of Epiphany. The calendar allowed these exotic, somewhat fairy-tale personages but a single day of presence beside the child's crib. And yet, in contrast to the attraction they had for us children, their message has to do with wisdom and faith; it is a message for adults.

Human wisdom, wonderfully developed through centuries of searching and attainment, is able to recognize the sign of God in the areas of its knowledge. The presence of the Magi tells us that it is not simplicity alone that attains to God but also the thirst for knowledge. The call of God is hidden even in the wonder and scandal of his creation. "They opened their treasures": their understanding and their heart. Thus the little statues of the Magi that we knew in childhood now loom large in our familiar crèches as admirable and much-loved ancestors who drew near to the divine mystery through the greatness and dignity of human wisdom.

I cannot pass over Herod, the other major character having to do with the crèche on this final day, before the slaughter of the innocents. In fact, Jerusalem with its towers, walls, and domes is always in the background of our crèches. And Jerusalem means power. Like wisdom, human power has the means of obtaining knowledge, and to it, too, God sends his signals. The intellectuals at the court hastened to put this power on guard. But power, unlike wisdom, is a one-way street: Its path is marked by cunning and pride, that is, by fear.

The Baptism That Calls for Courage

(The Baptism of the Lord)

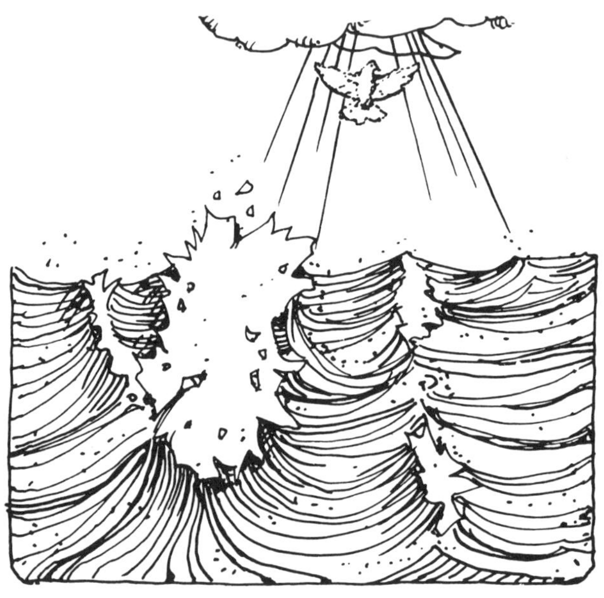

As the people were in expectation, and all men questioned in their hearts concerning John, whether perhaps he were the Christ, John answered them all, "I baptize you with water; but he who is mightier than I is coming, the thong of whose sandals I am not worthy to untie; he will baptize you with the Holy Spirit and with fire. . . ."

Now when all the people were baptized, and when Jesus also had been baptized and was praying, the heaven was opened, and the Holy Spirit descended upon him in bodily form, as a dove, and a voice came from heaven, "Thou art my beloved Son; with thee I am well pleased."

(Luke 3:15-16; 21-22)

***

Don Lorenzo Milani once said to producer Maurice Cloche, when urging him to make a movie about the life of Christ: "It's a strange thing, but today it is easier for people to believe that Jesus is God than to believe that he is a human being. The movie ought to make utterly clear what it means concretely to say that 'the Word became flesh.'" Taking the baptism of Jesus as an example of his humanity, Don Milani suggested showing that "Jesus is there, but he is so much a human being that he cannot be singled out from among the others."

This revolutionary approach compels us, whose Christianity is so much a matter of habit, to try to see Jesus as his contemporaries saw him, to see him with unprejudiced, completely new eyes. In this group on the banks of the Jordan are John and Jesus, but no one identifies Jesus as the Messiah; rather "all men questioned in their hearts concerning John, whether perhaps he were the Christ." By his anonymity here, by letting himself be taken for just another man, Jesus shows us how to be recognized as children of God: by submission, humility, complete availability as a servant among servants.

Here we find, once again, that Jesus came to overturn the worldly values on which we rely for our happiness. Unfortunately, none of us remembers his or her own baptism with water, because it was others who asked this great gift for us. Each of us, however, ought to have the courage to ask for, and live, the baptism "with the Holy Spirit and with fire." I say "the courage" because we may not forget that Jesus himself more than once uses the word "baptism" to describe his passion and death. Our second baptism awaits us at every turning point in our lives. Then it will be up to us as ordinary people, people anonymous as Jesus was at the Jordan, to decide, in the first person and in our very flesh, what answer we are to give to God's call.

Let Us Be Alive

(Second Sunday of the Year)

On the third day there was a marriage at Cana in Galilee, and the mother of Jesus was there; Jesus also was invited to the marriage, with his disciples. When the wine failed, the mother of Jesus said to him, "They have no wine." And Jesus said to her, "O woman, what have you to do with me? My hour has not yet come." His mother said to the servants, "Do whatever he tells you."

Now six stone jars were standing there, for the Jewish rites of purification, each holding twenty or thirty gallons. Jesus said to them, "Fill the jars with water." And they filled them up to the brim. He said to them, "Now draw some out, and take it to the steward of the feast." So they took it. When the steward of the feast tasted the water now become wine, and did not know where it came from (though the servants who had drawn the water knew), the steward of the feast called the bridegroom and said to him, "Every man serves the good wine first; and when men have drunk freely, then the poor wine; but you have kept the good wine until now." This, the first of his signs, Jesus did at Cana in Galilee, and manifested his glory; and his disciples believed in him.

(John 2:1-11)

***

We busy, preoccupied people burn our days one after another like matches. If someone were suddenly to ask us, "But what do you do to encounter Christ in your life?" we would be confused, surprised, somewhat irritated, and grieved: "I do nothing, exactly nothing, but where am I to find the time? Even more, where am I to find the opportunity?" Our life is made up of so many things, all of them necessary but also anonymous and of little interest; anything on a grand scale, like encountering Christ, seems so disproportionate, so absurd, that we have long since ceased even to think of it. Besides, where could I ever encounter him? Surely not in this house or this office or on these streets? As people dejected by experience, we smile at the thought. After all, you know what life is like!

But where could we possibly meet Christ if not in our everyday life? Nothing extraordinary happened at Cana: a marriage, a wedding feast, a little rejoicing, a few glasses more than one had intended. That's all there was. There is something almost scandalous about this first miracle of Jesus: more wine so as not to cut short the rejoicing of these people who were already somewhat tipsy!

Does everything, then, and I mean absolutely everything, take place in the presence of God? Our wretched days, our meager joys, our little sufferings? Yes, absolutely everything. Yet we are scandalized that even one glass too much of wine can help make evident God's presence at our side. "Grace is everywhere": These are the splendid words of the little priest of Ambricourt with which Bernanos ends his *Diary of a Country Priest.* We are not called to exceptional deeds but to live our ordinary life attentively. Sometimes I ask myself: How many at that banquet recognized the presence of God in their midst?

Ashes and Diamonds

(Third Sunday of the Year)

Inasmuch as many have undertaken to compile a narrative of the things which have been accomplished among us, just as they were delivered to us by those who from the beginning were eyewitnesses and ministers of the word, it seemed good to me also, having followed all things closely for some time past, to write an orderly account for you, most excellent Theophilus, that you may know the truth concerning the things of which you have been informed. . . .

And Jesus returned in the power of the Spirit into Galilee, and a report concerning him went out through all the surrounding country. And he taught in their synagogues, being glorified by all.

And he came to Nazareth, where he had been brought up; and he went to the synagogue, as his custom was, on the sabbath day. And he stood up to read; and there was given to him the book of the prophet Isaiah. He opened the book and found the place where it is written:

"The Spirit of the Lord is upon me, because he has anointed me to preach good news to the poor. He has sent me to proclaim release to the captives and recovering of sight to the blind, to set at liberty those who are oppressed, to proclaim the acceptable year of the Lord."

And he closed the book, and gave it back to the attendant, and sat down; and the eyes of all in the synagogue were fixed on him. And he began to say to them, "Today this scripture has been fulfilled in your hearing."

(Luke 1:1-4; 4:14-21)

***

Last Sunday, I found myself thinking that a Christian's legs, even if a bit weary, are like those of an old donkey: They may be ailing but they carry us to church on Sundays and allow us to say at least this in the Lord's presence: "Here I am!" On many occasions, I have gotten to the last Mass of our weekly feastday as the sun was setting or when it was already dark, and, carried there more by my legs than my heart, I have sat down in my usual corner with my spirit still oppressed by the preceding week and already burdened with the concerns of the week ahead.

You know what I mean: We sit there in our corner and wait. Then someone comes forward and proclaims to us the Word of God, the Gospel, the testimony that is the fruit of the "careful investigation" which Luke assures us he made of the treasures handed down, and this precisely in order that we might have the highest degree of certainty regarding what we hear. And then, as we sit there feeling oppressed, with souls perhaps no better disposed than those of the Nazarenes toward Jesus when he rose and read like a regular scribe, we too hear the "glad tidings": liberation for prisoners, sight for the blind, freedom for the oppressed.

Oppression and grace: two things opposed as darkness and light. Our oppression, our blindness, our daily imprisonment are pierced by grace. The Word of God reaches us in our apathy and calls us to life. Then, if we are not deaf and unbelieving, as the inhabitants of Nazareth were, we will arise from our chair and leave our corner; our legs will become nimbler, our spirits more joyous. We will not return home empty handed.

At the End of an Icy Road

(Presentation of the Lord)

When the time came for their purification according to the law of Moses, they brought Jesus up to Jerusalem to present him to the Lord (as it is written in the law of the Lord, "Every male that opens the womb shall be called holy to the Lord") and to offer a sacrifice according to what is said in the law of the Lord, "a pair of turtledoves, or two young pigeons."

Now there was a man in Jerusalem, whose name was Simeon, and this man was righteous and devout, looking for the consolation of Israel, and the Holy Spirit was upon him. And it had been revealed to him by the Holy Spirit that he should not see death before he had seen the Lord's Christ. And inspired by the Spirit he came into the temple; and when the parents brought in the child Jesus, to do for him according to the custom of the law, he took him up in his arms and blessed God and said, "Lord, now lettest thou thy servant depart in peace, according to thy word; for mine eyes have seen thy salvation which thou hast prepared in the presence of all peoples, a light for revelation to the Gentiles, and for glory to thy people Israel."

(Luke 2:22-33)

***

The Russians call it "The House of God." I am talking of the old folks' home. There was a time when I used to pay frequent visits to the V. . . Institute, sixty kilometers from Milan. The road to it runs through a flat countryside lined with mulberry trees; in winter the fields are white with frost, and in summer they are covered with corn. The old people are there, waiting. But it is not just children or relatives that they await. Their expectation is greater and more unconditional.

I can't remember which feastday it was, but on one occasion a little altar had been set up in the corridor on the first floor of the infirmary wing. The sister had prepared it carefully with a snow-white embroidered cloth and two large vases of red flowers at the sides. In utter silence the priest raised the host at the consecration. The doors of the rooms were opened wide, and each inmate could see the host from his or her own bed or from a wheelchair. These elderly people had raised themselves on their pillows in order to see the host; some had pulled themselves to the doors of their rooms. They looked at the host with childlike surprise and almost with yearning, as if they wanted to touch it.

Today, the words of the elderly Simeon, who waited an entire life to be able to take the child Jesus in his arms, this child that was the hope and salvation of the human race, remind me of those old people who appeared along the corridor of the infirmary carrying the burdens, anxieties, and joys of an entire life. Like Simeon, they were able to see God present among them, within arm's reach. You must forgive me, for in this passage of Luke I can see only the face of an old man as he repeats his hope-filled words: "Lord, now lettest thou thy servant depart in peace, according to thy word; for mine eyes have seen thy salvation."

In the Depths of the Night

(Fifth Sunday of the Year)

While the people pressed upon Jesus to hear the word of God, he was standing by the lake of Gennesaret. And he saw two boats by the lake; but the fishermen had gone out of them and were washing their nets. Getting into one of the boats, which was Simon's, he asked him to put out a little from the land. And he sat down and taught the people from the boat.

And when he had ceased speaking, he said to Simon, "Put out into the deep and let down your nets for a catch." And Simon answered, "Master, we toiled all night and took nothing! But at your word I will let down the nets." And when they had done this, they enclosed a great shoal of fish; and as their nets were breaking, they beckoned to their partners in the other boat to come and help them. And they came and filled both boats, so that they began to sink. But when Simon Peter saw it, he fell down at Jesus' knees, saying, "Depart from me, for I am a sinful man, O Lord." For he was astonished, and all that were with him, at the catch of fish which they had taken; and so also were James and John, sons of Zebedee, who were partners with Simon. And Jesus said to Simon, "Do not be afraid; henceforth you will be catching men." And when they had brought their boats to land, they left everything and followed him.

(Luke 5:1-11)

***

There once was a man who was very sad. It seemed to him that his life in its present form was worthless. He arose in the morning sad, and he went to bed in the evening sad. During the day he worked to support his family. He was married and had children. His earnings were barely sufficient, but at least they were enough. His days slipped by one after another, as did his weeks and months and years. His children grew up; he kept on working and gradually felt himself becoming an old man. There's no cure for it, he thought; when one worry ends, another begins; I toil, but my hands remain always empty. Therefore he was sad. His life seemed to him to be like a net; whenever he threw it into the water, it came up empty.

One night, when he was so tortured by despair that he could not sleep, he got up and, for the first time in many years, opened the Gospel and read: " 'Master, we toiled all night and took nothing! But at your word I will let down the nets.' And when they had done this, they enclosed a great shoal of fish." At this point, the man suddenly seemed to understand: The nets are full or empty depending on whether or not we let them down in the name of the Lord. Then, for the first time, he felt an intense joy and, suddenly, a great fear. He too had been a sinner until this moment, because he had lived in despair. And when, as he continued reading, he reached the words, "Do not be afraid," he began to weep there in the depths of the night, in the darkness of his house. He had understood that all human beings must see their condition, whatever it be, as God's will for them and that life has value only if it is lived with trust in God's Word. Everything else is unimportant and is to be thrown aside like a useless burden—even what we foolishly call "our life."

*''O that today you would
hearken to his voice!
Harden not your hearts.''*
(Ps 95:7-8)

Lent and the Resurrection of the Lord

The Man in Gray

(First Sunday of Lent)

Jesus, full of the Holy Spirit, returned from the Jordan, and was led by the Spirit for forty days in the wilderness, tempted by the devil. And he ate nothing in those days; and when they were ended, he was hungry. The devil said to him, "If you are the Son of God, command this stone to become bread." And Jesus answered him, "It is written, 'Man shall not live by bread alone.' "

And the devil took him up, and showed him all the kingdoms of the world in a moment of time, and said to him, "To you I will give all this authority and their glory; for it has been delivered to me, and I give it to whom I will. If you, then, will worship me, it shall all be yours." And Jesus answered him, "It is written, 'You shall worship the Lord your God, and him only shall you serve.' "

And he took him to Jerusalem, and set him on the pinnacle of the temple, and said to him, "If you are the Son of God, throw yourself down from here; for it is written, 'He will give his angels charge of you, to guard you,' and 'On their hands they will bear you up, lest you strike your foot against a stone.' " And Jesus answered him, "It is said, 'You shall not tempt the Lord your God.' " And when the devil had ended every temptation, he departed from him until an opportune time.

(Luke 4:1-13)

***

How poor we are, now that we no longer experience temptation! Really poor, because this means that we are diminished and impoverished in soul. If someone were to ask us whether we are ever tempted in the course of our day, we would be puzzled how to answer. No (it seems we must say), no, not really; no real temptations. Little thoughts, yes; things that do not count. We like the quiet life, the stagnant pools of apathy. In fact, the petition at the end of the Our Father seems to us almost exaggerated, if not useless: "And lead us not into temptation."

No, the devil is no longer part of our lives; he has no time to waste on us, or we on him. We are disappointed in each other. True enough, the world is full of crime as never before; people are everywhere killing one another; somewhere—who knows where?—further slaughter is being planned. But all this seems to us terribly natural; everything can be so easily and cynically explained by the kind of social and political analysis at which we have become experts that any presence of the devil in all this seems really improbable and, in fact, we never even think of it.

But if the devil does not occur to us, neither, I fear, does God. Our souls are no longer familiar with shadow and light but only with an unrelieved drab gray. In fact, we have for some time been subject to a single great but unrealized temptation: the suicide of the soul. We are killing ourselves without help, through asphyxiation. Contrasting colors hurt our eyes, and we can endure them only in the movies or on television. Good and evil are mixed together and becoming ever less distinguishable; evil is justifiable and goodness open to criticism. We even want to enter into paradise en masse, with closed eyes. God grant we may not all unwittingly find ourselves in hell.

What a Bore Perfection Is

(Second Sunday of Lent)

Jesus took with him Peter and John and James, and went up on the mountain to pray. And as he was praying, the appearance of his countenance was altered, and his raiment became dazzling white. And behold, two men talked with him, Moses and Elijah, who appeared in glory and spoke of his departure, which he was to accomplish at Jerusalem. Now Peter and those who were with him were heavy with sleep but kept awake, and they saw his glory and the two men who stood with him.

And as the men were parting from him, Peter said to Jesus, "Master, it is well that we are here; let us make three booths, one for you and one for Moses and one for Elijah"—not knowing what he said. As he said this, a cloud came and overshadowed them; and they were afraid as they entered the cloud. And a voice came out of the cloud, saying, "This is my Son, my Chosen; listen to him." And when the voice had spoken, Jesus was found alone. And they kept silence and told no one in those days anything of what they had seen.

(Luke 9:28b-36)

***

There are passages of the Gospel that somehow inspire joy and a good spirit. That, at least, has been my experience: I read them and find myself smiling. The passage from Luke that we have before us today is one such. Now—you may say—at first sight there is no reason here to smile; the passage tells us of nothing less than the transfiguration of Jesus in prayer, his glory and renewed acknowledgement as Son of God, and his "departure," which is announced as happening soon. And yet, in the background, behind this lofty tone, there is to be heard in the passage a kind of lower tone, I would even dare say, a comic tone: I am referring to the behavior of the apostles and especially of Peter. All right, let me say it openly: It is precisely their clumsiness, their failure to understand, their missing of the point, that opens my heart and makes me rejoice.

Yes, we ourselves are decidedly like those poor fellows: When everything seems to be going the right way, they want it to continue forever; they are sleepy and do not know what they are saying; their eyes open wide when they see their master's glory. We are the same: Ready to be either enthusiastic or despondent, we would like our moments of well being to be everlasting and our life to be lived in a kind of limbo in which there would be no more joys or sorrows. And, immediately after being raised to the heights, we are quick to take fright as soon as a cloud of unknown origin casts its shadow over our life. Faced with the greatness and mystery of God we are comic, inconstant creatures, somewhat slow witted, just like Peter, James, and John. But we shouldn't be discouraged. Smile and move on. Be generous and don't take ourselves too seriously.

Eternal Life Begins Yesterday

(Third Sunday of Lent)

There were some present at that very time who told Jesus of the Galileans whose blood Pilate had mingled with their sacrifices. And he answered them, "Do you think that those Galileans were worse sinners than all the other Galileans, because they suffered thus? I tell you, No; but unless you repent you will all likewise perish. Or those eighteen upon whom the tower in Siloam fell and killed them, do you think that they were worse offenders than all the others who dwelt in Jerusalem? I tell you, No; but unless you repent you will all likewise perish."

And he told this parable: "A man had a fig tree planted in his vineyard; and he came seeking fruit on it and found none. And he said to the vinedresser, 'Lo, these three years I have come seeking fruit on this fig tree, and I find none. Cut it down; why should it use up the ground?' And he answered him, 'Let it alone, sir, this year also, till I dig about it and put on manure. And if it bears fruit next year, well and good; but if not, you can cut it down.' "

(Luke 13:1-9)

***

The Gospel is not intended to frighten us; neither is life. When faced with seemingly inexplicable tragedies, such as entire countries obliterated by natural disasters, or indiscriminate butcheries, or sudden calamities striking whole families or children whom, in our superstitious idea of sin, we regard as more innocent than other people—how often in these cases we ask ourselves: "Why these people? Why at this moment in their lives?" And we are gripped by fear and depression. But the question, like the one asked by the Galileans, is based on an error, just as is our fear of death. Because we cling to life like shipwrecked people in a storm, death seems to us, no matter at what age it comes, to be an absurdity, an event that opens an abyss under a life which we can justify only with difficulty and sometimes cannot justify at all. We view death as absurd or, at best, as the beginning of a more real life, one of consolation, one at last fulfilled and happy, which we describe as eternal.

As long as we do not look at death and especially at life with new eyes, we will "all likewise" die a death that is absurd, like the eighteen who perished beneath the tower of Siloam or like all the people who die without reason in events that seem to us cruel and meaningless. In reality, we can and must overcome death here and now and immediately; we can begin our eternal life this very day. This is the good news, the Gospel for today: not depression and fear, but joy and fullness of life. We must bear fruit as long as we are planted in the soil of the earth; otherwise what is the difference between life and death, between a barren fig tree and a fig tree that has been pruned? We will find the barrenness of death within us even during what we call life, "unless we repent." On the other hand, death will not be able to rob us of anything if we have already turned our life into eternal life.

Like Tired Warriors

(Fourth Sunday of Lent)

Now the tax collectors and sinners were all drawing near to hear Jesus. And the Pharisees and the scribes murmured, saying, "This man receives sinners and eats with them." So he told them this parable:

"There was a man who had two sons; and the younger of them said to his father, 'Father, give me the share of property that falls to me.' And he divided his living between them. Not many days later, the younger son gathered all he had and took his journey into a far country, and there he squandered his property in loose living. And when he had spent everything, a great famine arose in that country, and he began to be in want. So he went and joined himself to one of the citizens of that country, who sent him into his fields to feed swine. And he would gladly have fed on the pods that the swine ate; and no one gave him anything. But when he came to himself he said, 'How many of my father's hired servants have bread enough and to spare, but I perish here with hunger! I will arise and go to my father, and I will say to him, "Father, I have sinned against heaven and before you; I am no longer worthy to be called your son; treat me as one of your hired servants."' And he arose and came to his father.

"But while he was yet at a distance, his father saw him and had compassion, and ran and embraced him and kissed him. And the son said to him. 'Father, I have sinned against heaven and before you; I am no longer worthy to be called your son.' But the father said to his servants, 'Bring quickly the best robe, and put it on him; and put a ring on his hand, and shoes on his feet; and bring the fatted calf and kill it, and let us eat and make merry; for this my son was dead, and is alive again; he was lost, and is found.' And they began to make merry.

"Now his elder son was in the field; and as he came and drew near to the house, he heard music and dancing. And he called one of the servants and asked what this meant. And he said to him, 'Your brother has come, and your father has killed the fatted calf, because he has received

him safe and sound.' But he was angry and refused to go in. His father came out and entreated him, but he answered his father, 'Lo, these many years I have served you, and I never disobeyed your command; yet you never gave me a kid, that I might make merry with my friends. But when this son of yours came, who has devoured your living with harlots, you killed for him the fatted calf!' And he said to him, 'Son, you are always with me, and all that is mine is yours. It was fitting to make merry and be glad, for this your brother was dead, and is alive; he was lost and is found.' "

(Luke 15:1-3, 11-32)

***

To which of the two sons in the parable do we feel closer: the prodigal son, or the son who never left his father's house? If we habit-bound Christians resemble either of them, surely it is the elder son, this creature without any strange ideas in his head but also without generosity or good impulses. His father actually has to explain to him in detail why there should be a feast; the fellow is unable to understand it on his own. What conclusion follows from all this? A simple one: there is more joy in forgiving and being forgiven than in having nothing to forgive. In fact, this last is an unreal and improbable situation; it is proof of a lack of love and perhaps of mistrust of oneself and of others.

Am I defending sin, then? No, I am pleading for repentance and forgiveness. We need both of these at every moment. I am pleading that we must be adults and leave behind childhood and fear. When we accept risks, we will indeed suffer and even make mistakes, but we will also have great opportunities to experience in our own flesh how it is permissible to run great risks but also how difficult and even impossible it is to cope with these risks if we assume that we have nothing more to do with our Father's house, that we are self-sufficient. Only if we take risks will we discover the true nature of our mistakes and feel the need of forgiveness. And this forgiveness will be granted us, out of love and love alone and in a measure that is generous beyond anything we had hoped for.

Those, on the other hand, who through mistrust or fear dare not risk their possessions (which are always the Father's possessions) will inevitably believe that the Father's possessions belong to them; they will be jealous and live with heads bowed to the ground. They will never know the grandeur of repentance and forgiveness or surrender their own treasure for the treasure common to all.

Those Useless Stones in Our Hands

(Fifth Sunday of Lent)

Jesus went to the Mount of Olives. Early in the morning he came again to the temple; all the people came to him, and he sat down and taught them. The scribes and the Pharisees brought a woman who had been caught in adultery, and placing her in the midst they said to him, ''Teacher, this woman has been caught in the act of adultery. Now in the law Moses commanded us to stone such. What do you say about her?'' This they said to test him, that they might have some charge to bring against him. Jesus bent down and wrote with his finger on the ground. And as they continued to ask him, he stood up and said to them, ''Let him who is without sin among you be the first to throw a stone at her.'' And once more he bent down and wrote with his finger on the ground. But when they heard it, they went away, one by one, beginning with the eldest, and Jesus was left alone with the woman standing before him. Jesus looked up and said to her, ''Woman, where are they? Has no one condemned you?'' She said, ''No one, Lord.'' And Jesus said, ''Neither do I condemn you; go, and do not sin again.''

(John 8:1-11)

***

I have frequently asked myself why people are so often unhappy. Or, more accurately, so vexed and oppressed. And the more unhappy, vexed, and oppressed they are in spirit, the more the dark shadow of evil seems to grow and fill the horizon, invading everything to the point of seeming invincible. How much suffering there is, how much injustice and crime and butchery! "How much evil there is in the world!" we exclaim in moments of depression. "How much evil there is in human beings!" Then, as though hypnotized by this dark, despairing vision, we turn our gaze upon ourselves and confess: "How much evil there is in me!" Conscious of our sins we withdraw with bowed heads, like the men who wanted to stone the adulteress.

Is the world, then, so sunk in sin that no other judgment is possible? Is there no relief from our sense of oppression? Will we never be free of it? But it is precisely at this point of our depression that the Gospel presents itself with good news: Sin disappears under the gaze of Christ; our wretched tribunals melt away as did the crowd of would-be stoners, and we are left alone with Christ. There we hear to our astonishment that sin is not a reason for condemnation but only a sign that we have strayed from the path of true life. There we hear that an escape from our sense of oppression is not only possible but is here before us and indeed already within us: "Go, and do not sin again."

There, under the redemptive gaze of Christ, evil is already conquered for good. Its terribleness, which according to the Law makes it subject to death (by stoning), is suddenly seen to be a wretched little thing, not only not calling for judgment upon us but already condemned and overcome. We are immediately sent back to live our life but now with a new outlook, as men and women who have been converted, and not as guilty parties. It is all so simple: Christ asks us not to waste time along the way, and sin is often simply a stupid waste of time.

The Clamor of the Mute

(Palm Sunday)

And when Jesus had said this, he went on ahead, going up to Jerusalem. When he drew near to Bethphage and Bethany, at the mount that is called Olivet, he sent two of the disciples saying, "Go into the village opposite, where on entering you will find a colt tied, on which no one has ever yet sat; untie it and bring it here. If any one asks you, 'Why are you untying it?' you shall say this, 'The Lord has need of it.' " So those who were sent went away and found it as he had told them. And as they were untying the colt, its owners said to them, "Why are you untying the colt?" And they said, "The Lord has need of it."

And they brought it to Jesus, and throwing their garments on the colt they set Jesus upon it. And as he rode along, they spread their garments on the road. As he was now drawing near, at the descent of the Mount of Olives, the whole multitude of the disciples began to rejoice and praise God with a loud voice for all the mighty works they had seen, saying, "Blessed is the King who comes in the name of the Lord! Peace in heaven and glory in the highest!"

And some of the Pharisees in the multitude said to him, "Teacher, rebuke your disciples." He answered, "I tell you, if these were silent, the very stones would cry out."

(Luke 19:28-40)

***

The voice. Have we ever asked ourselves what use we make of our voices? Except for the time we spend sleeping, there is no moment of the day when we are not using words. The voices of the human race—excited, chaotic, demanding, lively, despairing—cover the world with a net that is inescapable, turbulent, as compact as our desires, as violent as our passions. And yet in reality it is as if silence weighed upon the world and upon our days: All our wretched noise passes away, and our voices, along with the sentiments that impelled them, are lost; our days are empty and, under the noise, desperately silent. Any festive spirit, any joy, likewise vanishes, and we are left mute, dumbfounded, dissatisfied. Our voices sound unreal in the box that is the world, like the sound of a movie or a noisy television spectacle that no longer exists the moment we turn up the lights or press a button.

The part God plays in our daily life is so impoverished, so submerged, that even his name never reaches our lips and we have nothing to say about his presence in our lives. If the thought of God comes to mind, it is a fugitive, almost shapeless thought that never reaches the point of being voiced. Silence about God: a silence that oppresses us and makes each succeeding day more burdensome, each succeeding minute more intolerable. Yet we continue to remain silent. No one dares speak of God. Our society that is so garrulous has exiled God as an improper subject in our dealings with one another, a subject that cannot be suitably combined with everything else. Therefore we say nothing of him and speak of other things. We warble away skillfully enough, but no voice is raised to speak of God. Our Christianity is mute. Therefore the sentence at the end of today's Gospel is meant for us: "If these were silent, the very stones would cry out."

Every Day Is Easter

(Easter Sunday)

Now on the first day of the week Mary Magdalene came to the tomb early, while it was still dark, and saw that the stone had been taken away from the tomb. So she ran, and went to Simon Peter and the other disciple, the one whom Jesus loved, and said to them, "They have taken the Lord out of the tomb, and we do not know where they have laid him." Peter then came out with the other disciple, and they went toward the tomb. They both ran, but the other disciple outran Peter and reached the tomb first; and stooping to look in, he saw the linen cloths lying there, but he did not go in. Then Simon Peter came, following him, and went into the tomb; he saw the linen cloths lying, and the napkin, which had been on his head, not lying with the linen cloths but rolled up in a place by itself. Then the other disciple, who reached the tomb first, also went in, and he saw and believed; for as yet they did not know the scripture, that he must rise from the dead.

(John 20:1-9)

***

It is true: The days of our lives slip away uniformly, and we cannot reconcile ourselves to the fact. We are always looking for something new and decisive to happen, something that will radically change our lives from those of human beings who are half-asleep and weighed down by an invisible stone into lives in which every action and every minute will have a meaning and be worth living. We get up in the morning and look at the sky: It is raining; is that the sun? We open the newspapers: Nothing there, nothing of what we are unconsciously waiting for, no good news for us. The day passes, evening returns, we are still waiting: Nothing decisive has happened; we are simply a day older. We go to bed, and before closing our eyes, we abandon ourselves, only half-awake, to the groundless hope that tomorrow will really be an "other," different day.

We live through an endless Lent, an endless time of waiting, but our Easter, our Pasch, or "passage," seems never to come. And yet today is Easter, today Christ is risen, today the stone has been rolled from the tomb and death has been overcome. Today our waiting is over. But have we enough faith to believe that this is true each and every day? Since that distant morning every day is the day of our resurrection; every day the stone that seals the tomb of our life is rolled away and we can truly rise. The news is that the joy of Easter can be our daily joy. We need not wait any longer; we need not wait for another day, for everything has already happened and we are free. This freedom is the gift given us by the resurrection: the victory over our fears small and great, the liveliness and joy of a new life. Nothing has changed around us and yet everything is new; we need no longer depend on anything or anyone for our joy, for we have rolled away the stone.

I Doubt, Therefore I Am Alive

(Second Sunday of Easter)

On the evening of that day, the first day of the week, the doors being shut where the disciples were, for fear of the Jews, Jesus came and stood among them and said to them, "Peace be with you." When he had said this, he showed them his hands and his side. Then the disciples were glad when they saw the Lord. Jesus said to them again, "Peace be with you. As the Father has sent me, so I send you." And when he had said this, he breathed on them, and said to them, "Receive the Holy Spirit. If you forgive the sins of any, they are forgiven; if you retain the sins of any, they are retained."

Now Thomas, one of the twelve, called the Twin, was not with them when Jesus came. So the other disciples told him, "We have seen the Lord." But he said to them, "Unless I see in his hands the print of the nails, and place my finger in the mark of the nails, and place my hand in his side, I will not believe."

Eight days later, his disciples were again in the house, and Thomas was with them. The doors were shut, but Jesus came and stood among them, and said, "Peace be with you." Then he said to Thomas, "Put your finger here, and see my hands; and put out your hand, and place it in my side; do not be faithless, but believing." Thomas answered him, "My Lord and my God!" Jesus said to him, "Have you believed because you have seen me? Blessed are those who have not seen and yet believe."

(John 20:19-29)

***

We are on Thomas' side, on the side of both his unbelief and his faith. To say that we are on Thomas' side is not to deny the truth and difficult exhortation contained in the words of Jesus: "Blessed are those who have not seen and yet believe." It is simply choosing to be honest. To be honest with God means to make faith the center of our life. Our time passes amid countless occupations and preoccupations; one day, at a still proximate or perhaps now long-distant point in our lives, we said yes or no to God, and we tried to believe that the choice was irreversible. Our contention with God stopped there; we did not speak of it again or discuss it again with him. We have not dared to say to him: "No, I deceived myself or perhaps I deceived you. My heart is full of pain, but today I am no longer able to believe in you." Neither, on the other hand, have we fallen on our knees and cried out an impassioned profession of faith. Anesthetized in blind rejection or in a fidelity we dare not question, we live out the days of our life like sleepwalkers.

To be honest with God means bringing faith to bear on every occasion; it means experiencing the joy of feeling it grow or the pain of seeing it diminish like a stream that retreats and leaves our soul high and dry. But honesty with God also extends to the anguish of doubt, the risk of losing in order to gain everything. Faith is not money that one buries to keep it from being stolen; it is a treasure used with some risk in order to make it grow constantly. To be on Thomas' side, then, means to suffer from our unbelief but also to acknowledge that unbelief so that some day we will be able to throw it at Christ's feet and cry, "My Lord and my God!"

The Right Side of the Boat

(Third Sunday of Easter)

After this Jesus revealed himself again to the disciples by the Sea of Tiberias; and he revealed himself in this way. Simon Peter, Thomas called the Twin, Nathanael of Cana in Galilee, the sons of Zebedee, and two others of his disciples were together. Simon Peter said to them, "I am going fishing." They said to him, "We will go with you." They went out and got into the boat; but that night they caught nothing.

Just as day was breaking, Jesus stood on the beach; yet the disciples did not know that it was Jesus. Jesus said to them, "Children, have you any fish?" They answered him, "No." He said to them, "Cast the net on the right side of the boat, and you will find some." So they cast it, and now they were not able to haul it in, for the quantity of fish. That disciple whom Jesus loved said to Peter, "It is the Lord!" When Simon Peter heard that it was the Lord, he put on his clothes, for he was stripped for work, and sprang into the sea. But the other disciples came in the boat, dragging the net full of fish, for they were not far from the land, but about a hundred yards off.

When they got out on land, they saw a charcoal fire there, with fish lying on it, and bread. Jesus said to them, "Bring some of the fish that you have just caught." So Simon Peter went aboard and hauled the net ashore, full of large fish, a hundred and fifty-three of them; and although there were so many, the net was not torn. Jesus said to them, "Come and have breakfast." Now none of the disciples dared ask him, "Who are you?" They knew it was the Lord.

Jesus came and took the bread and gave it to them, and so with the fish. This was now the third time that Jesus was revealed to the disciples after he was raised from the dead.

When they had finished breakfast, Jesus said to Simon Peter, "Simon, son of John, do you love me more than these?" He said to him, "Yes, Lord; you know that I love you." He said to him, "Feed my lambs." A second time he said to him, "Simon, son of John, do you love me?" He said to him, "Yes, Lord; you know that I love you." He said to him, "Tend my sheep." He said to him the third time, "Simon, son of John, do you love me?" Peter was grieved because he said to him the third time, "Do you love me?" And he said to him, "Lord, you know everything; you know that I love you.'' Jesus said to him, ''Feed my sheep. Truly, truly, I say to you, you girded yourself and walked where you would; but when you are old, you will stretch out your hands, and another will gird you and carry you where you do not wish to go.'' (This he said to show by what death he was to glorify God.) And after this he said to him, ''Follow me.''

(John 21:1-19)

***

We may be tempted to say that we too would like to see a fire burning on the shores of our daily, fishless lake, on the shores of our desolation and solitude. After the difficult but exciting years of following Jesus on the roads and in the villages of Palestine, and after the terrible days of the recent Passover, the disciples seem to have returned, bewildered and perhaps disappointed, to the daily occupations and life that they had left with hearts full of hope. Why had they bothered leaving these everlastingly empty nets if now they had to return to them on a chilly morning like all the other mornings of their lives and to cast them into the water and pull them out empty once more? Their hearts are so oppressed that they do not even recognize Jesus speaking to them.

We are like them; we too drag out our days with bowed heads, preoccupied with our own concerns, and we do not recognize the presence of Christ in the little incidents that occur in our lives precisely while we are most caught up in the laborious task of earning a living. But if we have kept a sense of expectation alive in our hearts, then indeed a fire is lit on the beach; we recognize the familiar signs, and our daily activities, so emptied of significance by repetition and routine, take on meaning once more. If expectation is not dead in our hearts, the great moment will always come, the moment so longed for and so feared: the moment for changing our lives. For there is always a right side of the boat where the fish teem. Then, like Peter, we shall at once throw ourselves into the water and hear again the voice that urges us to start living again and to love without reservation (see the great, repeated declaration of love that is asked of Peter). We shall hear again the unsurpassable words we thought we were incapable of ever hearing again: ''Follow me.''

Those Saints Sitting and Waiting

(Fourth Sunday of Easter)

"My sheep hear my voice, and I know them, and they follow me; and I give them eternal life, and they shall never perish, and no one shall snatch them out of my hand. My Father, who has given them to me, is greater than all, and no one is able to snatch them out of the Father's hand. I and the Father are one."

(John 10:27-30)

***

Eternal life. What does it mean when I or anyone else says: I shall have eternal life? And why the future tense: I shall have? We are so used to thinking of our eternity as a state that awaits us after death, a hope that will open up for us in the future, that we fail to note the unmistakably clear words of Christ: "I give them eternal life." Eternal life, therefore, is here and now; it is not a reward that awaits us after life is done, nor a state of which we shall know nothing until we have passed through the inevitable narrow passage of death.

But how can my life, my poor little life, be so wretched and at the same time already eternal? That was the thought that came to me as I looked at the bodies sitting and waiting in the outpatient department at Niguarda. It was the department of cosmetic surgery, and each person was sitting there with their own affliction: children who had burned their hands in their childish games; men with arms and legs burned during their terrible adult labors. All sat there with infinite patience, waiting for the nurse to emerge through a green curtain and call their names. The nurse would appear at the curtain and call a name; a person would get up, make his way through the room, and disappear behind the curtain. If a child's name was called, it was frequently a woman who would get up, and the child in her arms would cling to her hand and begin to cry.

"Eternal life," I thought. "Eternal life for each of them. And for me too, here and now, in this hospital waiting room, this place of anxieties, hopes, and sufferings." I could not have explained why the thought came to me at that moment and in that situation, but it did come to me, and I wanted to cry out to each of them—those workers, those mothers: "All of us—you, I, your children—all possess eternal life." A life whose every moment is of eternal value, a life available to each person in the endless throng of everyday saints.

Free from Fear

(Fifth Sunday of Easter)

When Judas had gone out, Jesus said, "Now is the Son of man glorified, and in him God is glorified; if God is glorified in him, God will also glorify him in himself, and glorify him at once. Little children, yet a little while I am with you. . . . A new commandment I give to you, that you love one another; even as I have loved you, that you also love one another. By this all men will know that you are my disciples, if you have love for one another."

(John 13:31-33a, 34-35)

***

Is it really possible for us to love one another? Yet this is the one commandment, the only explicit request—a new commandment that includes all the others—that Christ has left us. But whom are we to love, and how are we to love?

We are so riddled with prejudices and interior conflicts and we have built our lives on divisions to such an extent that we find it almost impossible to approach others without suspicion, without seeing them as probable enemies, or without fear. Our relations with others are falsified: We want immediately to pigeonhole them, label them, find out to what extent and in what ways they resemble or differ from us and our accustomed way of looking at the world and evaluating ourselves. We see and fear in others what is different from us, what might cause a crisis for us or fail to acknowledge the image which we have formed of ourselves and without which we would find life impossible. We are prisoners of ourselves, of our past, our convictions, our habits.

The commandment of love that Christ lays upon us is thus one more spur to freedom, for only those who are free can love. His commandment is an urgent call to cast out fear, for it is only the fearful who are unable to love. If we were in fact free of all limiting conditions, but especially of fear, all reservations and all the distinctions dictated by a false prudence and wisdom would automatically vanish. We would no longer ask how and whom we must love, because we would no longer be worried about preserving our narrow individual lives; we would no longer feel separated from anything or anyone.

Christ's commandment is "new" precisely because it takes a "new human being" to put it into practice. If we achieve that degree of newness, the snares which we have laid for ourselves will fall away. Christ's teaching on the eve of his glorification is not a different or higher teaching than he had given earlier; it represents simply the natural state of those who become his followers. For in fact "by this all men will know that you are my disciples."

The Peace of Warriors

(Sixth Sunday of Easter)

Jesus answered him, "If a man loves me, he will keep my word, and my Father will love him, and we will come to him and make our home with him. He who does not love me does not keep my words; and the word which you hear is not mine but the Father's who sent me.

"These things I have spoken to you, while I am still with you. But the Counselor, the Holy Spirit, whom the Father will send in my name, he will teach you all things, and bring to your remembrance all that I have said to you. Peace I leave with you; my peace I give to you; not as the world gives do I give to you. Let not your hearts be troubled, neither let them be afraid. You heard me say to you, 'I go away, and I will come to you.' If you loved me, you would have rejoiced, because I go to the Father; for the Father is greater than I. And now I have told you before it takes place, so that when it does take place, you may believe."

(John 14:23-29)

***

''You wanted my peace. Come and take it!'' These challenging words mark the end of Georges Bernanos' first and splendid novel, *Under the Sun of Satan.* The elderly priest, whom the people dub ''The Saint of Lumbres'' and who is modeled on the Cure of Ars, has been taken by death in his confessional. ''Like a sentry killed by a bullet in his sentry-box,'' is what the successful author said of him when he came down from Paris, himself a restless spirit, to see and taste the sweetness of the much-touted Christian peace that might be found in the existence of a holy country priest. And indeed he found this peace with all its unexpected violence, all its immense challenge, in the darkness of a confessional box that closed like a grave around the body of a poor priest who, almost against his will, dared to set out on the rough road of holiness.

Christian peace. What on earth is this peace that is not the kind which ''the world gives,'' but is something different? How stupidly jealous the world is of this peace! Have you never seen them look at you with sheeps' eyes, with a smile hovering between melancholy and envy, and heard them say to you in moments of adversity, distress, and apprehension, ''But you're a Christian; you have your faith and your peace.'' It's as if they were saying: ''You're tough skinned and do not feel the sting of your wounds; your peace, which is the peace of Christ, preserves you like an impregnable breastplate.'' In fact, how pleasant a Christian's life is—according to the world!

''To bestow this peace which is never experienced when sought for its own sake'': That is another sentence from Bernanos. Precisely because the peace which Christ has left us is not the peace of this world, it is not a state of happiness, much less of insensitivity; rather, it is a peace ''despite'' distress and suffering; it is the certainty that nothing is lost.

If You Cannot Walk, Fly

(The Ascension of the Lord)

Jesus said to them, "Thus it is written, that the Christ should suffer and on the third day rise from the dead, and that repentance and forgiveness of sins should be preached in his name to all nations, beginning from Jerusalem. You are witnesses of these things. And behold, I send the promise of my Father upon you; but stay in the city, until you are clothed with power from on high."

Then he led them out as far as Bethany, and lifting up his hands he blessed them. While he blessed them, he parted from them and was carried up into heaven. And they worshiped him and returned to Jerusalem with great joy, and were continually in the temple praising God.

(Luke 24:46-53)

***

Once again there is the question of changing one's life. In fact, that is precisely the message which Jesus leaves with the apostles as he ascends to heaven: "conversion and the forgiveness of sins." After all, what does "to be converted" mean if not to direct one's steps along the way pointed out by Christ and to forget any other possible way?

How often in the course of our lives, and even in the course of a single day, have we not said to ourselves: "No, I can't go on this way; I just have to change." We don't know what it is that has to change, but change there must be. Then in our apprehension we sift through our days, trying to see where and how we have gone astray. Like a train that suddenly comes to the end of the line out in the open countryside, we try to retrace our steps. But our life is the result of a countless number of individual choices made at every moment and in every kind of circumstance. It is impossible to travel the path in reverse and undo it.

That is not how a conversion takes place; that is not how one changes one's life. Only by accepting the fact that we have come to a dead end, only by acknowledging and, I might even say, blessing God for our despair, can we discover that the cage in which we thought ourselves trapped has in fact no bars. The same choices that caused us to founder can become the instrument of our conversion. It will be as if we had learned to fly. There are no more obstacles; everything is truly grace, that is, a means of salvation. At this point the second part of Christ's message—"the forgiveness of sins"—becomes clear. Conversion also does away with all sin, that is, with all wandering along uncertain ways. If everything is grace, then straying is no longer part of our life, and the cross of the risen Christ casts its shadow over all of the past and all of the future.

I Have Tried the World: It Is Tasteless

(Pentecost)

On the evening of that day, the first day of the week, the doors being shut where the disciples were, for fear of the Jews, Jesus came and stood among them and said to them, ''Peace be with you.'' When he had said this, he showed them his hands and his side. Then the disciples were glad when they saw the Lord. Jesus said to them again, ''Peace be with you. As the Father has sent me, so I send you. . . . Receive the Holy Spirit. If you forgive the sins of any, they are forgiven; if you retain the sins of any, they are retained.''

(John 20:19-21, 23)

***

"I send you." And we go; like it or not, we go: inferior messengers, often sad and unworthy messengers, but messengers nonetheless. Many of us have forgotten the message received and have gone about with empty hands, messengers without a message. And yet the world is still there, daily waiting outside the door of the house. No, I take that back: The world that awaits the message of Christ begins within the walls of our own house, our own room, our own heart. The bearer of the message knows no limits or space or time for its proclamation: The mission begins here and now and continues everywhere and always. Therefore, carrying no special baggage (as the Gospel bids) and wearing no sign to set us apart (not even a priest's cassock, for example) because the message has been entrusted to all of us without distinction, we daily traverse the streets as conscious or forgetful witnesses to Christ.

The day is long, our tasks are many and wearisome, and many are the parts we play in the complex game of life: father or mother, husband or wife, son or daughter, friend, fellow worker, companion on a journey or on the streets, or simply an anonymous passerby. Each of us has many roles and many responsibilities, but the ultimate meaning of each of our actions is that we are messengers of Christ. The mandate seems so impossibly difficult to carry out that we have ghettoized it, as it were, entrusting it to others and retaining for ourselves the role of bored spectators on Sundays when the priest once again proclaims the Gospel to us from the altar. We have forgotten that we ourselves, in the first person, must be the salt of the earth or else become parents without true parenthood, children without hope, mute companions, friends with no gifts to give, and insubstantial shadows in a world which we uselessly complain has lost all its savor.

It Was There, Right Before His Eyes

(Trinity Sunday)

"I have yet many things to say to you, but you cannot bear them now. When the Spirit of truth comes, he will guide you into all the truth; for he will not speak on his own authority, but whatever he hears he will speak, and he will declare to you the things that are to come. He will glorify me, for he will take what is mine and declare it to you. All that the Father has is mine; therefore I said that he will take what is mine and declare it to you."

(John 16:12-15)

***

"He will guide you into all the truth." "What is truth?" Pilate asked (John 18:38). The question hides an infinite weariness, an element of disconcerting honesty. Imagine Pilate in all his poor, limited power, all his shrewdness as an administrator, all his clear-eyed despair as a human being, whispering this question to himself rather than to Jesus. He had Jesus before him and was questioning him, and yet he did not know what truth was. But then not even the apostles, who had experienced so many moments of enthusiasm and disappointment with Jesus and had seen his miracles and heard his words—not even they, gathered now for the final meal, had attained possession of the truth.

We too, after almost two thousand years of Christianity, find ourselves bewildered as we ask ourselves: "What about me? Do I perhaps know what truth is? Do I pass my life, my days, in the light of truth, or do they rather slip away, as chance or sad habit decides, in a cloud that does not let me see what is before my eyes?" What did Pilate and the apostles, what do we, lack that would enable us to know the truth? After all, we have all encountered Christ. The truth is there before us as it was before Pilate, but we do not see it. We know the Gospel, we hear it every Sunday in our churches, and yet we remain unbelievably stupid. We listen but do not understand.

Like the apostles, we need the "Spirit of truth," that is, the light without which we see without seeing and hear without understanding. With that Spirit we will understand what remained dark to Pilate: that Christ and the truth are not two separate things; Christ *is* the truth. "He will glorify me." There is, therefore, but one truth: the truth which Christ incarnated when he came among us and which the Spirit will help us to recognize and make our own each day.

The Crowd in the Subway

(Corpus Christi)

Jesus welcomed the crowds and spoke to them of the kingdom of God, and cured those who had need of healing. Now the day began to wear away, and the twelve came and said to him, "Send the crowd away, to go into the villages and country round about, to lodge and get provisions; for we are here in a lonely place." But he said to them, "You give them something to eat." They said, "We have no more than five loaves and two fish— unless we are to go and buy food for all these people." For there were about five thousand men. And he said to his disciples, "Make them sit down in companies, about fifty each." And they did so, and made them all sit down. And taking the five loaves and the two fish he looked up to heaven, and blessed and broke them, and gave them to the disciples to set before the crowd. And all ate and were satisfied. And they took up what was left over, twelve baskets of broken pieces.

(Luke 9:11-17)

***

"For we are here in a lonely place." A crowd in a lonely place: But isn't that an everyday sight? That is what I asked myself as I descended to the main level of the subway. I was used to the scene, since each day, at the beginning and end of the day's work, I plunge, like thousands of others, into the swarming subterranean world that has become the symbol of our collective life of good and evil, especially now that suicides have become more numerous down there than ever before. I asked myself why people should take their lives right in the middle of a crowd. Why, if not to prove their extreme, intolerable loneliness?

Then I tried to look at these anonymous frequenters of the subway as a series of individuals, and I saw that each of them carried their own life around with them as they did the clothing they had put on: negligently, almost with boredom. Each seemed to dislike himself or herself as well as other people. They let themselves be carried up and down by the escalators; they crowded the platforms behind the yellow danger lines; they crammed together in the cars and sat there or stood clinging to the support straps: each empty faced, each sunk as it were in some distant thought, some remote hope, some hunger forever unsatisfied. Each of these bodies was hungry, hungry for an unknown food to which no one could even have given a name. They were indeed a hungry crowd in a lonely place. And they were afraid.

Then, in my distress I imagined that the miracle was repeated, that the forgotten tabernacles of the entire city were thrown open and someone descended with that bit of bread to feed this throng; and I was sure that all would have enough to satisfy themselves and that for once at least they would know what it means not to be hungry.

Man shall not live by bread alone,
but by every word that proceeds from the mouth of God.
(Matt 4:4)

Sundays and Feasts

Miracles at the Door of the House

(Tenth Sunday of the Year)

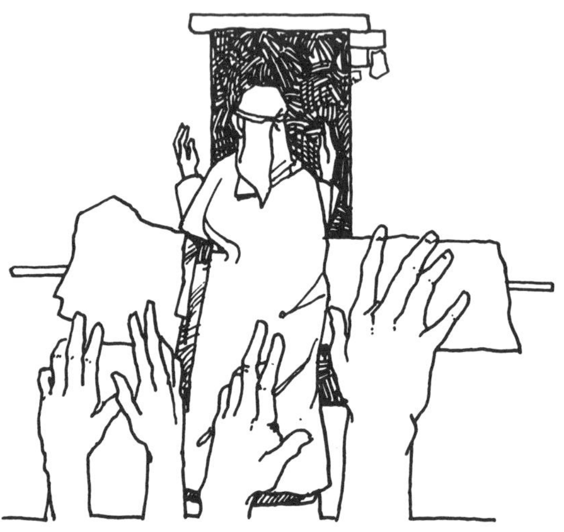

Soon afterward Jesus went to a city called Nain, and his disciples and a great crowd went with him. As he drew near to the gate of the city, behold, a man who had died was being carried out, the only son of his mother, and she was a widow; and a large crowd from the city was with her. And when the Lord saw her, he had compassion on her and said to her, "Do not weep." And he came and touched the bier, and the bearers stood still. And he said, "Young man, I say to you, arise." And the dead man sat up, and began to speak. And he gave him to his mother. Fear seized them all; and they glorified God, saying, "A great prophet has risen among us!" and "God has visited his people!" And this report concerning him spread through the whole of Judea and all the surrounding country.

(Luke 7:11-17)

***

Not because of any special predisposition she possesses nor because of some timid act of faith but simply because she is a suffering human being who has been touched by tragedy, this mother of Nain is found worthy of a divine intervention. In an instant, solely by reason of the divine favor, she suddenly passes from despair to joy. That's right, we haven't misunderstood: simply in order that she might not have to mourn any longer.

The disturbing presence of Christ reaches us and saves us daily amid joys (do you recall the wedding at Cana and the affectionate but seemingly "useless" miracle of the wine?) and amid sorrows (isn't it just as useless to raise a dead person? We know that water will never be wine and that, no matter what, human beings are always fated to die). The miracles of Christ are first and foremost signs of the unbroken presence of God in the history of the human race, but they are also the flashing out of that presence before our closed eyes. Life is made up of joys and sorrows, and whether we realize it or not, everything is under the gaze of God. "God has visited his people!" the crowd exclaims. This is the discovery, the illumination, that occurs now as then.

Even if we do not think we have ever witnessed a miracle, each of us has experienced the presence of God at certain moments in our lives; we have felt it near, sharing in our poor human history. Each of us has had his or her eyes opened, even if only for a moment. It is, of course, only our blindness that keeps us from seeing the presence of God in even the smallest incidents in which we take part each day. The things that we in our insensitivity are willing to acknowledge and proclaim as "miracles" are happening around us at every moment. Every life is made up of hidden miracles; we are always on the road that leads through Nain.

Fear Passed Off as Common Sense

(Eleventh Sunday of the Year)

One of the Pharisees asked Jesus to eat with him, and he went into the Pharisee's house, and sat at table. And behold, a woman of the city, who was a sinner, when she learned that he was sitting at table in the Pharisee's house, brought an alabaster flask of ointment, and standing behind him at his feet, weeping, she began to wet his feet with her tears, and wiped them with the hair of her head, and kissed his feet, and anointed them with the ointment.

Now when the Pharisee who had invited him saw it, he said to himself, "If this man were a prophet, he would have known who and what sort of woman this is who is touching him, for she is a sinner." And Jesus answering said to him, "Simon, I have something to say to you." And he answered, "What is it, Teacher?" "A certain creditor had two debtors; one owed five hundred denarii, and the other fifty. When they could not pay, he forgave them both. Now which of them will love him more?" Simon answered, "The one, I suppose, to whom he forgave more." And he said to him, "You have judged rightly." Then turning toward the woman he said to Simon, "Do you see this woman? I entered your house, you gave me no water for my feet, but she has wet my feet with her tears and wiped them with her hair. You gave me no kiss, but from the time I came in she has not ceased to kiss my feet. You did not anoint my head with oil, but she has anointed my feet with ointment. Therefore I tell you, her sins, which are many, are forgiven, for she loved much; but he who is forgiven little, loves little." And he said to her, "Your sins are forgiven." Then those who were at table with him began to say among themselves, "Who is this, who even forgives sins?" And he said to the woman, "Your faith has saved you; go in peace."

(Luke 7:36-50)

***

"People capable of love, under the present system, are necessarily the exceptions; love is by necessity a marginal phenomenon in present-day Western society." So speaks philosopher Erich Fromm in his book *The Art of Loving*. The power of loving is becoming the most difficult one for the soul to exercise. So true is this that today, as never before, books and manuals claiming to teach what love is and how to love and become lovable are all the rage. For example, is there anyone who has not picked up *Infatuation and Love* by Alberoni, a sociologist, or has not at least heard tell of it? Anyone who has not had recourse to the advice of a man named Buscaglia? And if we fall back on people like Buscaglia, then the sickness is really serious.

We must therefore start all over again: We no longer know how to love, and this is suddenly frightening us. But have human beings ever been able to love? The words of Jesus to the Pharisees constantly ring in our Christian ears as a scorching rebuke. If loving means emerging from our self-centeredness and risking our entire selves without calculating the cost and without expecting anything in return, if it means being capable of generous feeling that may seem even silly in the eyes of the world, then we are no longer able to love. Selfishness, fear, common sense, have turned us into cold-blooded animals.

We are extremely skilled in the modern science of "public relations" and, like the Pharisee in the Gospel, remain on very excellent terms of good fellowship. But we are not prepared to go beyond common sense, beyond a respect which we claim is mutual. Even the plea to be forgiven, forgiven at every moment and in every action of our lives, seems excessive to us. What is there for which I need forgiveness! And we reach the point of asking ourselves: Is there really such a thing as sin? No, perhaps sin no longer exists for us; our inability to love has killed even our capacity for sinning and being forgiven.

Losing in Order to Save

(Twelfth Sunday of the Year)

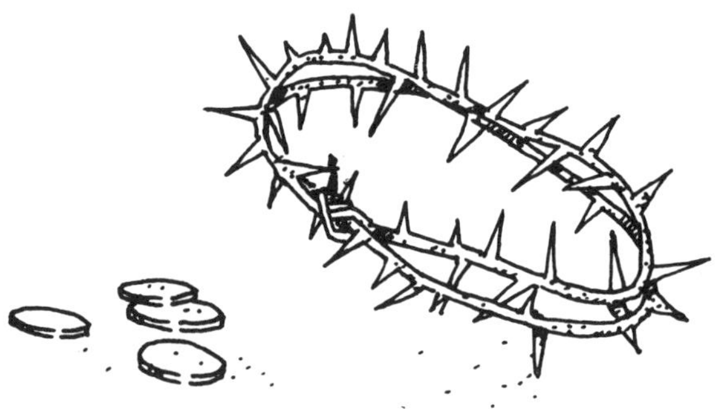

Now it happened that as Jesus was praying alone the disciples were with him; and he asked them, "Who do the people say that I am?" And they answered, "John the Baptist; but others say Elijah; and others, that one of the old prophets has risen." And he said to them, "But who do you say that I am?" And Peter answered, "The Christ of God." But he charged and commanded them to tell this to no one, saying, "The Son of man must suffer many things, and be rejected by the elders and chief priests and scribes, and be killed, and on the third day be raised."

And he said to all, "If any man would come after me, let him deny himself and take up his cross daily and follow me. For whoever would save his life will lose it; and whoever loses his life for my sake, he will save it."

(Luke 9:18-24)

***

"Whoever would save his life . . . .": But isn't that what we are doing every day? I have nothing against insurance policies. Some are necessary, others obligatory; the fact remains that we do nothing else each day but protect our life and our possessions. I myself have insured my life; every time I think of it I laugh, but the fact is that I did it. Am I therefore a sinner? Perhaps I am.

I still recall my first visit long ago to the offices of the insurance company. It was a touching scene. They made me lie on a bed; they listened to my heart and lungs, took my blood pressure, looked for hidden tumors, wanted to know whether I drank too much, whether there had been suicides in my family, and other pleasant facts. They wanted to be sure they were making a good investment or, in short, that I would not die the next day, right after the contract had been signed. I haven't died, but I feel myself to be nonetheless an impostor because I am selling what I do not possess, since, after all, who can go surety for even a hair ot his head? Who can go surety for his own life for a year or a day or an hour? And yet—or rather for that very reason—we all insure our lives and in practice do not even think of not doing so; we are ready to do a good many things, not all of them admirable, to guarantee our security.

Despite all this, how often we hear people say or say ourselves: "I have thrown my life away; I am throwing my life away." What does this mean? Haven't we carefully shored it up on every side? Not at all! We acknowledge to some extent that the props are still there but also that the life is no longer there; the existence we all drag out daily is no longer life. And then, what a mess have I not put together, my God? The answer is to be found in the words which Jesus says to "all" at the end of today's Gospel.

A Body in Order to Remain Alive

(Feast of Sts. Peter and Paul, Apostles)

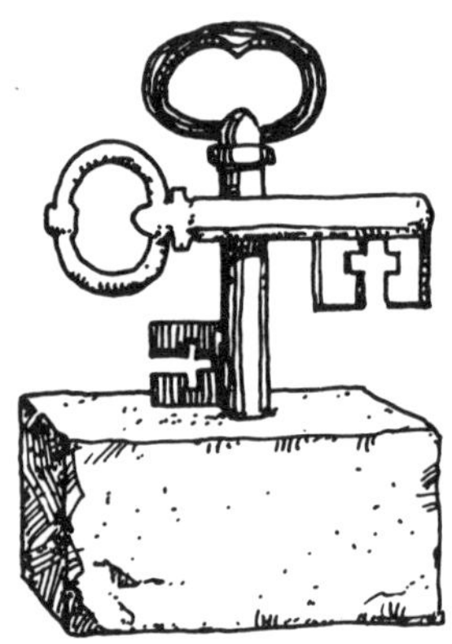

Now when Jesus came into the district of Caesarea Philippi, he asked his disciples, "Who do men say that the Son of man is?" And they said, "Some say John the Baptist, others say Elijah, and others Jeremiah or one of the prophets." He said to them, "But who do you say that I am?" Simon Peter replied, "You are the Christ, the Son of the living God." And Jesus answered him, "Blessed are you, Simon Bar-Jona! For flesh and blood have not revealed this to you, but my Father who is in heaven. And I tell you, you are Peter, and on this rock I will build my church, and the powers of death will not prevail against it. I will give you the keys of the kingdom of heaven, and whatever you bind on earth shall be bound in heaven, and whatever you loose on earth shall be loosed in heaven."

(Matt 16:13-16)

***

The recognition of Jesus as Messiah and sole hope of salvation is inseparable from recognition of the Church as the one body in which human beings are to live in order to make the kingdom of God a reality. We are often tempted, however, to reduce Christianity to a personal bent of soul, a private sentiment. Christianity is not a sentiment at all. Love of parents or children, even love of neighbor can be a sentiment; Christianity cannot.

How often we have heard people say with the air of one expressing an especially intelligent conviction: "I accept and love Christ but not his Church. I manage my relationship with Christ on my own without intermediaries." We do not realize that when we take this approach we are reducing Christ, the God who became flesh, to a God without a body, an abstraction made in our image and likeness. We turn Christ into an ideal to which we can only aspire as to an unachievable perfection. But Christ is not at all an ideal, and Christians are not idealists. Christians are concrete persons, each with a name and a surname, who live here and now and have a part to play in God's plan of salvation, a plan that embraces everyone and is brought to fulfillment by the daily efforts of each of us.

It has been said that no one is saved by himself or herself. We need the Church as we need a body in order to remain alive and not be reduced to ghosts. Don Lorenzo Milani wrote, "I will never rebel against the Church, because several times a week I need forgiveness for my sins, and I would not know to whom I could turn for that forgiveness if I left the Church." This introduces a concreteness that may seem even scandalous to some refined souls. But, then, Christianity is a scandal.

All Those Stairs

(Fourteenth Sunday of the Year)

After this the Lord appointed seventy others, and sent them on ahead of him, two by two, into every town and place where he himself was about to come. And he said to them, "The harvest is plentiful, but the laborers are few; pray therefore the Lord of the harvest to send out laborers into his harvest. Go your way; behold I send you out as lambs in the midst of wolves. Carry no purse, no bag, no sandals; and salute no one on the road. Whatever house you enter, say first, 'Peace be to this house!' And if a son of peace is there, your peace shall rest upon him; but if not, it shall return to you. And remain in the same house, eating and drinking what they provide, for the laborer deserves his wages; do not go from house to house. Whenever you enter a town and they receive you, eat what is set before you; heal the sick in it and say to them, 'The kingdom of God has come near to you.' But whenever you enter a town and they do not receive you, go into its streets and say, 'Even the dust of your town that clings to our feet, we wipe off against you; nevertheless know this, that the kingdom of God has come near.' I tell you, it shall be more tolerable on that day for Sodom than for that town. . . ."

The seventy returned with joy, saying, "Lord, even the demons are subject to us in your name!" And he said to them, "I saw Satan fall like lightning from heaven. Behold, I have given you authority to tread upon serpents and scorpions, and over all the power of the enemy; and nothing shall hurt you. Nevertheless, do not rejoice in this, that the spirits are subject to you; but rejoice that your names are written in heaven.''

(Luke 10:1-12, 17-20)

***

I remember the time when we tried to put this section of the Gospel into practice in our parish, a large one in the innermost suburban circle around Milan. The ''laborers'' were truly not numerous: four priests, including the pastor, for a thousand families. The statistics told a clear story: The Word of God in the form of the Sunday Gospel reached only a small number of these families, if it reached even them. The majority never came to church except for baptisms and funerals, and all did not come even then. As far as these last were concerned, even the hasty ''birthday blessing'' did not reach them.

The priests were too few to knock on every door. What of other workers? We, a group of lay volunteers, tried to reach the majority. We abandoned all our baggage, that is, we who were professional people, housekeepers, workers, students, all sought to forget our varied training and experience and to be simply men and women who were bringing our own witness and the Word of God in the measure that each of us was capable. To our invitation that was left at every porter's lodge people replied in large numbers, perhaps from a desire to hear a different message, perhaps simply out of curiosity. I know that we climbed many sets of stairs and that I have never gotten to know any other neighborhood of my city as well as I did that one.

The fact is that most of these visits took the form of long hours of listening. People, we discovered, need to talk, to tell someone of their problems. And the problems were many and unsuspected. We visitors said little, but the mere fact of our presence in their homes was meant to give them confidence, to tell them they were not alone, to tell them some hope was still possible. We cured no one, we reduced no demon to subjection. Perhaps we did not even return full of joy, but we did return convinced more than ever that the harvest was plentiful.

On the Road

(Fifteenth Sunday of the Year)

And behold, a lawyer stood up to put Jesus to the test, saying, "Teacher, what shall I do to inherit eternal life?" He said to him, "What is written in the law? How do you read?" And he answered, "You shall love the Lord your God with all your heart, and with all your soul, and with all your strength, and with all your mind; and your neighbor as yourself." And he said to him, "You have answered right; do this, and you will live."

But he, desiring to justify himself, said to Jesus, "And who is my neighbor?" Jesus replied, "A man was going down from Jerusalem to Jericho, and he fell among robbers, who stripped him and beat him, and departed, leaving him half dead. Now by chance a priest was going down that road; and when he saw him he passed by on the other side. So likewise a Levite, when he came to the place and saw him, passed by on the other side. But a Samaritan, as he journeyed, came to where he was; and when he saw him, he had compassion, and went to him and bound up his wounds, pouring on oil and wine; then he set him on his own beast and brought him to an inn, and took care of him. And the next day he took out two denarii and gave them to the innkeeper, saying, 'Take care of him; and whatever more you spend, I will repay you when I come back.' Which of these three, do you think, proved neighbor to the man who fell among the robbers?" He said, "The one who showed mercy to him." And Jesus said to him, "Go and do likewise."

(Luke 10:25-37)

***

"Go and do likewise." Could anything be clearer? This is one of the simplest parables and its meaning seems unmistakable. Ever since then we have stood with mouths hanging open, not knowing exactly what to do. Of course, if a situation turned up that was as clear as the one the Samaritan found himself in, we would not lose heart; even we would know where our duty lay. We would pick up our unknown neighbor from the roadside and spend an entire day of our sacred weekend or our crowded workday in order to carry him quickly to a place of help, stay with him, spend the night at his bedside, put our hand in our wallet, and, on returning from our ruined weekend or our perhaps spoiled business errand, spend the time telling ourselves that all was well. That, more or less, is what we would do. Are we sure? Of course we are; after all, it's not every day we have to pick someone up from beside the road! Come on! Even we would go that far, or just about.

But at this point there is something that has escaped us and is the very thing that makes the parable burdensome, the very thing that is its "snag." We have failed to see that the parable is really not limited; the seemingly exceptional situation is in fact a daily situation. The road from Jerusalem to Jericho is not our expressway (that would be too simple!); it is nothing less than the path of my own life, and the stricken man is I myself (I am my first "neighbor" if I am to love my neighbor as myself) and all the people I meet on this road, daily, in every situation, even the most ordinary and routine. All and each of us must bind up one another's wounds that life inflicts; we must have "compassion" on one another. To have compassion means to suffer together.

Slaves of Ourselves

(Sixteenth Sunday of the Year)

Now as they went on their way, Jesus entered a village; and a woman named Martha received him into her house. And she had a sister named Mary, who sat at the Lord's feet and listened to his teaching. But Martha was distracted with much serving; and she went to him and said, "Lord, do you not care that my sister has left me to serve alone? Tell her then to help me." But the Lord answered her, "Martha, Martha, you are anxious and troubled about many things; one thing is needful. Mary has chosen the good portion, which shall not be taken away from her."

(Luke 10:38-42)

***

Anxious and troubled. The words sound like a description of our souls, of our daily condition. But they also picture our society, in which illness becomes health and error virtue and in which the claim to be masters of life turns into the most burdensome slavery. On the other hand, why should I call it quits? Could I call it quits? If I did, I would in a moment be unhorsed, trampled on, and tossed aside to wither on the wreckage-strewn bank of that swirling river which sweeps our lives along. Anyone who stops is lost. One against all. What of the soul? But is there really an immortal soul? And if it really exists, what am I to do with it? I have no time to waste on what cannot be seen and touched. Nor is there any longer time and opportunity for charity, for compassion, for a hope that is not simply desire, for a love that is not possession, for a faith that is not routine, or worse, a hoarding of God.

Everything seems to be dried up by the ceaseless wind of anxiety. Desire has been renamed energy; our peace is in a bank account; our glory is identified with ambition; and understanding of human beings has been used to turn our neighbor into a tool. Is there anyone who has not seen a painting of the general judgment? All the movement is in the depiction of hell. In groups and singly, as though prey to a blind voluptuousness, souls hurl themselves toward their punishment, still driven by the excitation that marked their entire lives. Who could bring a single one of these souls to a halt? Anxiety has deafened them to any call whatsoever.

But (it will be said) you are exaggerating, for Martha, after all, sought only to make a good impression on Jesus. There you have the very root of the error. When will we stop trying to make a good impression even on God?

Waiting Under the Closed Window

(Seventeenth Sunday of the Year)

Jesus was praying in a certain place, and when he ceased, one of his disciples said to him, "Lord, teach us to pray, as John taught his disciples." And he said to them, "When you pray, say: 'Father, hallowed be thy name. Thy kingdom come. Give us each day our daily bread; and forgive us our sins, for we ourselves forgive every one who is indebted to us; and lead us not into temptation.' "

And he said to them, "Which of you who has a friend will go to him at midnight and say to him, 'Friend, lend me three loaves; for a friend of mine has arrived on a journey, and I have nothing to set before him'; and he will answer from within, 'Do not bother me; the door is now shut, and my children are with me in bed; I cannot get up and give you anything'? I tell you, though he will not get up and give him anything because he is his friend, yet because of his importunity he will rise and give him whatever he needs.

"And I tell you, Ask, and it will be given you; seek, and you will find; knock, and it will be opened to you. For every one who asks receives, and he who seeks finds, and to him who knocks it will be opened. What father among you, if his son asks for a fish, will instead of a fish give him a serpent; or if he asks for an egg, will give him a scorpion? If you then, who are evil, know how to give good gifts to your children, how much more will the heavenly Father give the Holy Spirit to those who ask him!"

(Luke 11:1-13)

***

I once knew a man who no longer prayed. One would be tempted to say that prayer had dried up in him like a plant without water; he had not watered the plant as he should have, and it was his fault that it died. At times we are even presumptuous enough to think that we are sinners in this matter. But that is not the case; with all our presumption we cannot cause even the smallest leaf to wither or grow green again on the plant with which we like to compare prayer. Prayer can blossom when we least expect it; sometimes even when everything is completely encased in ice. No one can judge his or her neighbor when it comes to prayer.

I once knew, then, a man who no longer prayed, or at least who was convinced he did not pray, just as all who no longer pray are convinced of it. And naturally, like all who no longer pray, he too would have liked to begin praying again. In other words, he had retained at least the seed of prayer, even if he did not know what to do with it. On Sundays he went to church and attended Mass, but he was unable to open his mouth; he could not utter even the Our Father. He listened with scrupulous attention as the faithful recited this prayer aloud, but he himself could not take any part in it, either in word or in spirit. The reason was not pride, for in fact he felt humiliated by his inability, nor was it indifference, for he suffered from it. He knew only that he must wait, hold on to the seed against all hope, and not throw it away. One day it would blossom again; he did not know when, since prayer itself is a gift, just like the three loaves in the Gospel, and one must wait stubbornly under the closed window.

That is what this man did: He waited, and this waiting upon prayer was already his prayer, though he did not realize it. I say this because today's Gospel reading is a reading about hope against any and all despair: a hope that is unqualified, stubborn, enormous.

Living Corpses

(Eighteenth Sunday of the Year)

One of the multitude said to Jesus, "Teacher, bid my brother divide the inheritance with me." But he said to him, "Man, who made me a judge or divider over you?" And he said to them, "Take heed, and beware of all covetousness; for a man's life does not consist in the abundance of his possessions." And he told them a parable, saying, "The land of a rich man brought forth plentifully; and he thought to himself, 'What shall I do, for I have nowhere to store my crops?' And he said, 'I will do this: I will pull down my barns and build larger ones; and there I will store all my grain and my goods. And I will say to my soul, Soul, you have ample goods laid up for many years; take your ease, eat, drink, be merry.' But God said to him, 'Fool! This night your soul is required of you; and the things you have prepared, whose will they be?' So is he who lays up treasure for himself, and is not rich toward God."

(Luke 12:13-21)

***

"Soul, take your ease." As if the soul could ever be at ease! Even worse: as if the soul could ever find peace in a secure abundance of material things! That is the mistake of the "rich man," and our mistake too: to turn values upside down and, by an absurd and deadly somersault, to set the dynamism of life on its head. To believe that our soul, the part of us that with good reason makes our life restless, could ever be rendered calm and quiet—and this by possessions. To abandon ourselves with full stomachs, overflowing hands, and replete minds to the dreams of body and spirit. Here everything has been silenced by reducing our bellies and our God to a system: our bellies with food, our God with observance of his precepts. For, just as we can amass food and money enough to deceive ourselves into thinking the future secure, so too we can deceive ourselves into thinking we pile up credit with God. By the shrewd use of my talents, the wily application of my powers, I reduce my earthly well being once and for all to a system; by my prudence, fidelity, and observance, without having to risk anything else, I claim to have provided myself with a secure place in eternal life.

But it is precisely at this moment that death intervenes, and not just the death of the body, as the parable seems to suggest, but that even more terrible death that turns us into living corpses. We eat, talk, walk about, and go dutifully to our churches, but in reality we are dead. Life has fled from us, and we haven't even noticed it, like the soldier Tolstoy describes who after being struck full in the chest during a battle continued to run about, thinking himself still alive. Life consists of movement and risk; a treasure that is buried yields no profit, a soul that has achieved complete calm wastes away. Let us ask God to keep us alert and ready, like athletes on the eve of a competition.

All the Lamps Lit

(Nineteenth Sunday of the Year)

Jesus said to his disciples, "Fear not, little flock, for it is your Father's good pleasure to give you the kingdom. Sell your possessions, and give alms; provide yourself with purses that do not grow old, with a treasure in the heavens that does not fail, where no thief approaches and no moth destroys. For where your treasure is, there will your heart be also.

"Let your loins be girded and your lamps burning, and be like men who are waiting for their master to come home from the marriage feast, so that they may open to him at once when he comes and knocks. Blessed are those servants whom the master finds awake when he comes; truly, I say to you, he will gird himself and have them sit at table, and he will come and serve them. If he comes in the second watch, or in the third, and finds them so, blessed are those servants! But know this, that if the householder had known at what hour the thief was coming, he would have been awake and would not have left his house to be broken into. You also must be ready; for the Son of man is coming at an hour you do not expect."

Peter said, "Lord, are you telling this parable for us or for all?" And the Lord said, "Who then is the faithful and wise steward, whom his master will set over his household, to give them their portion of food at the proper time? Blessed is that servant whom his master when he comes will find so doing. Truly, I tell you, he will set him over all his possessions. But if that servant says to himself, 'My master is delayed in coming,' and begins to beat the menservants and the maidservants, and to eat and drink and get drunk, the master of that servant will come on a day when he does not expect him and at an hour he does not know, and will punish him, and put him with the unfaithful. And that servant who knew his master's will, but did not make ready or act according to his will, shall receive a severe beating. But he who did not know, and did what deserved a beating, shall receive a light beating. Every one to whom much is given, of him will much be required; and of him to whom men commit much they will demand the more."

(Luke 12:32-48)

***

"Let us ask God to keep our souls alert and ready, like athletes on the eve of a competition." It was with these words that I ended last week's commentary. Now today's Gospel tells us: "Be ready, for the Son of man is coming at an hour you do not expect." Unfortunately, however, such appeals, instead of making us glad, abash and sadden us. We go away abashed because we are neglectful stewards and do not keep ourselves in readiness for meeting the returning master; we are saddened because our dismayed minds hasten ahead to the hour of our death.

But why on earth should Christ come only at the end of our life, as the words "The End" come at the close of a quite average movie? Why should he not come as the main scene, the one in which the whole meaning of our history is played out? For at the moment of his coming a decision is made on our life past and future, and "future life" includes not just our "heavenly" life but also and above all the rest of our "earthly" life: our life here and now. We need a great deal of attentiveness and watchfulness if we are to recognize his tread and go with lighted lamps to meet the master who is coming to call us. Then there shall be a moment of great rejoicing because our life will shift from expectation to joy, as our black-and-white film turns technicolored. This is quite a different outlook than just "thinking of death"!

But those who pass their lives in dreams or distractions or, even worse, in presuming on their own authority (the servant who beats his fellow servants), will not hear the call to true life. They shall certainly die, even if not yet in the body. But there is a further joy-giving lamp for today: Those presumptuous, know-it-all servants will be beaten as hard as possible, while the poor devils and the dull witted will get off with a few wallops. The wise are like the rich: Too fat to pass through, they must thin down. The poor and the simple will slip inside, even if they have to take a few cuffs on the head.

Drawing-Room Christians

(Twentieth Sunday of the Year)

"I came to cast fire upon the earth; and would that it were already kindled! I have a baptism to be baptized with; and how am I constrained until it is accomplished!

"Do you think that I have come to give peace on earth? No, I tell you, but rather division; for henceforth in one house there will be five divided, three against two and two against three; they will be divided, father against son and son against father, mother against daughter and daughter against her mother, mother-in-law against her daughter-in-law and daughter-in-law against her mother-in-law."

He also said to the multitudes, "When you see a cloud rising in the west, you say at once, 'A shower is coming'; and so it happens. And when you see the south wind blowing, you say, 'There will be scorching heat'; and it happens. You hypocrites! You know how to interpret the appearance of earth and sky; but why do you not know how to interpret the present time?"

(Luke 12:49-57)

***

Here is something strange: nowadays we Christians seem to get along well with everybody, and by and large, everybody gets along well with us. There was a time, as everyone knows, back at the beginning when it was not so. Otherwise there would not have been so many martyrs. It's not that I yearn for martyrdom, but this tranquillity of ours, this mutual tolerance we practice, seems suspect to me. Anything but fire and sword, anything but salt in the wounds! Fire scorches, the sword cuts, and salt burns in wounds.

There is something out of kilter here. But (you say) we live in a pluralistic, democratic country; everyone is free to practice his or her own religion; were we to act otherwise, that would be the last straw! Of course, but Athens too was a city open to every form of thought; everything could be discussed, and people were curious about everything and willing to listen even to a little Jew named Paul, a "semiliterate," as he spoke of his God and the need for the human race to change its ways. But when Paul came to what we would call the heart of the matter, the resurrection of Christ, they had had enough; they dismissed him with a sneer: "We will hear you again about this," and left him to himself.

So, then, Paul was completely unsuccessful in "good society" and among the big intellectuals of his day precisely because in the last analysis he took his stand on faith and forthrightly proclaimed the good news. He felt no need of being in agreement with the philosophers in the marketplace. I leave aside the fact that they took him for a madman. As for us, no one deserts us right in the middle of a drawing room; no one takes us for madmen; they do not lock us up in a lunatic asylum, which would be the logical step and which happens in some Eastern countries that, if nothing else, act more consistently with their own atheism.

The trouble is that we do not fully play our part as Christians; we do not proclaim our truth publicly and in its entirety. But then, why quarrel? What pleasure is there in making enemies? You never know, tomorrow you may need them all.

The Big Sad Eyes of God

(Twenty-first Sunday of the Year)

Jesus went on his way through towns and villages, teaching, and journeying toward Jerusalem. And some one said to him, "Lord, will those who are saved be few?" And he said to them, "Strive to enter by the narrow door; for many, I tell you, will seek to enter and will not be able. When once the householder has risen up and shut the door, you will begin to stand outside and knock at the door, saying, 'Lord, open to us.' He will answer you, 'I do not know where you come from.' Then you will begin to say, 'We ate and drank in your presence, and you taught in our streets.' But he will say, 'I tell you, I do not know where you come from; depart from me, all you workers of iniquity!' There you will weep and gnash your teeth, when you see Abraham and Isaac and Jacob and all the prophets in the kingdom of God and you yourselves thrust out. And men will come from east and west, and from north and south, and sit at table in the kingdom of God. And behold, some are last who will be first, and some are first who will be last."

(Luke 13:22-30)

***

The chosen of the Lord are an invisible folk. No one knows who they are. As we walk the streets of our city in the evening at the end of a tiring day, our unknown brothers and sisters throng together on the sidewalks, each with their own life, their own worries, their own immoderate or modest hopes. Our faces resemble one another, our bodies are alike, and yet each person conceals an essential, unique secret of which perhaps no one ever thinks. How many of us will be saved? Who? Why?

Will it perhaps be that preoccupied man, that smiling woman, the child playing there, that sullen, silent beggar? Will it perhaps be that policeman, or that Moroccan selling cigarette lighters, or that little girl on her bicycle, or that pale old man who looks as if he hadn't the strength to get anywhere? Which of them is knocking at that narrow door? Which of them will sit at table in the kingdom of God? It is Sunday: We enter a church and see people standing up, sitting, praying aloud, and gazing toward the altar. Are these perhaps among the saved?

Who the elect are has never been more unknown than today. Our East and West are no longer geographical sectors but a dimension of the heart and the spirit. We who are Christians by registration as infants and by habit suppose that we have a place waiting for us in the kingdom of God; we are so sure of it that we never even think about it; meanwhile the army of the unknown goes in ahead of us; those "last" of whom we know nothing force their way into the kingdom.

To All the Unknown Saints

(Twenty-second Sunday of the Year)

One sabbath when Jesus went to dine at the house of a ruler who belonged to the Pharisees, they were watching him. . . .

Now he told a parable to those who were invited, when he marked how they chose the places of honor, saying to them, "When you are invited by any one to a marriage feast, do not sit down in a place of honor, lest a more eminent man than you be invited by him; and he who invited you both will come and say to you, 'Give place to this man,' and then you will begin with shame to take the lowest place. But when you are invited, go and sit in the lowest place, so that when your host comes he may say to you, 'Friend, go up higher'; then you will be honored in the presence of all who sit at table with you. For every one who exalts himself will be humbled, and he who humbles himself will be exalted."

He said also to the man who had invited him, "When you give a dinner or a banquet, do not invite your friends or your brothers or your kinsmen or rich neighbors, lest they also invite you in return, and you be repaid. But when you give a feast, invite the poor, the maimed, the lame, the blind, and you will be blessed, because they cannot repay you. You will be repaid at the resurrection of the just."

(Luke 14:1, 7-14)

***

Once again we hear a warning that we shall perhaps not be first. An invisible throng, unknown to us but known to God, goes before us. Since the kingdom of God is open to all, we have not the slightest idea of what place we will have in the list. Those who presume that they know more are already on the wrong path and should prepare themselves to abandon their place of honor at the banquet.

We need only open the newspaper or turn on the television, and we will see the melting pot that simmers beneath our feet: a throng of lowly folk, of people unknown to the world, unknown likewise to our churches on Sundays. They are people we should never dare judge, because the hand of God is upon them as they live and end their lives in ways alien and mysterious to us, ways that have no place in our organization of things and in our prudential views.

I keep newspaper clippings as though they were the pages of a martyrology; I reread the names there as people read the names of the throngs of unknown saints in the breviary: a shepherd boy in Sardinia who grew tired of being humiliated and hung himself from a beam in the sheepfold; a vagrant who burned himself alive on the platform in Termini Station; two little girls who were raped because they had stolen some figs; four children who were buried when their wretched house collapsed on them at Torre del Greco; an unemployed Roman who killed himself out of shame at the most recent humiliation he had suffered; a mother who threw herself and her two youngest children under a train, after telling the oldest girl, who was eleven, "Go away, you can take care of yourself."

Not all such individuals crowd the pages of the newspapers; the majority live and disappear unknown to most people, with a simple faith of which we have no experience. I have jotted down their names, and as I wait for the streetcar or the subway, I glance through the pages of this new breviary: Cataldo, Salvatore, Cinzia, Antonella, Guglielmo, Giuseppe, Adriano, Concetta, Maria . . . pray for us.

So Many Little Gods

(Twenty-third Sunday of the Year)

Now great multitudes accompanied Jesus; and he turned and said to them, "If any one comes to me and does not hate his own father and mother and wife and children and brothers and sisters, yes, and even his own life, he cannot be my disciple. Whoever does not bear his own cross and come after me, cannot be my disciple.

"For which of you, desiring to build a tower, does not first sit down and count the cost, whether he has enough to complete it? Otherwise, when he has laid a foundation, and is not able to finish, all who see it begin to mock him, saying, 'This man began to build, and was not able to finish.' Or what king, going to encounter another king in war, will not sit down first and take counsel whether he is able with ten thousand to meet him who comes against him with twenty thousand? And if not, while the other is yet a great way off, he sends an embassy and asks terms of peace. So therefore, whoever of you does not renounce all that he has cannot be my disciple."

(Luke 14:25-33)

***

Instead of heeding Jesus we love ourselves. What I mean is that we cannot live without an image of ourselves that allows us to be self-satisfied. That is the lesson taught us by the kind of psychology and psychoanalysis that is sold for a song on every street corner by impromptu gurus: To be happy we must overcome all interior conflict; our life must be made up of actions that are always rewarding; we must allow no uncertainties in our behavior and therefore must enjoy an income that is comfortable and, above all, unaccompanied by any sense of guilt. We like to see in our mirrors the image of a winner, no matter how many dead or wounded we may have left on the field: the weaker, the more scrupulous. That is the law at work in survival on the playing field and in the cheerful abuse of power. It's useless and bad for you to feel remorse; the sole purpose of conscience is to give us back the certainty of our own powers.

Yes, they have taught us to love ourselves without limit along with our vices and sins; these, of course, are no longer known as vices and sins but simply as "the ego," that is, "I," "I," "I." Woe to those who do not love themselves! Our personalities are machines perfectly adapted to winning. Therefore we can no longer endure doubt and defeat; therefore we are so terribly fragile. With the aid of the instruction books on how to be a success we become apprentices for suicide. For, if neither the analysts nor the instruction books will save us, who or what can save us? We have become our own only and ultimate god. For the sake of this dreadful divinity human beings waste their best energies in learning and loving a success that in fact has nothing lovable about it.

Jesus bids us hate this false, self-conceited, and laughable way of life, just as he calls upon us to hate attachment to material things and even to family affections when these are looked upon as objects to be possessed, as things that make us rich and satisfied, or to put it differently, blind and deaf. He calls upon us to wake up and to dislodge the false values of the world from their pedestal.

Between Elevator and Subway

(Feast of the Exaltation of the Cross)

Jesus said to Nicodemus, "No one has ascended into heaven but he who descended from heaven, the Son of man. And as Moses lifted up the serpent in the wilderness, so must the Son of man be lifted up, that whoever believes in him may have eternal life."

For God so loved the world that he gave his only Son, that whoever believes in him should not perish but have eternal life. For God sent the Son into the world, not to condemn the world, but that the world might be saved through him.

(John 3:13-17)

***

For us the cross is a sign of salvation, the sign that we have been saved. At one time it was customary— and I hope it still is, with some people at least—to begin and end the day with the sign of the cross. A person who makes this sign awakens in the morning like the captain of a ship who quickly reviews his situation as he brushes his teeth and drinks his first cup of coffee. The sign of the cross shows us where we are, just as on diagrams of large complexes a red dot shows us our present location. With this as my starting point I must advance, I must make decisions and take actions that affect my own life and the lives of others.

My day, my daily adventure, the span of time within which, now and then, I risk everything—my earthly fortune and my eternal life—starts with this sign. It may do so only at the last moment, while on the landing I await the whistling sound of the elevator and the car that opens and sucks me down toward the street, toward the world, toward my known or anonymous neighbors; just at that point, with my briefcase clutched in one hand, with the other I sign myself with the sign of the cross: in the name of the Father and of the Son and of the Holy Spirit. And away I go, Amen! in the sign of the saving power that descends upon us in memory of the salvation which Christ, raised aloft on Calvary, came to bring to anyone who believes and makes of the cross not only the symbol but also the very means of his or her own salvation.

Is there anyone without a cross of their own? Some of us, in fact, are weighed down and exhausted by it; sometimes, each day is a cross. Then, like Simon of Cyrene we will submit to the burden; like the good thief we will go up there on the wood of pain and salvation, and we will say, "Remember me . . . ," and the reply will come back, "This very day. . . ." For prayer made through the cross meets no obstacles.

But that describes the heroic acceptance of the cross. For us poor Christians of the elevator and the subway it will be enough to end our day with this sign that is both remembrance and hope.

It Only Takes a Spark to Burn Down a House

(Twenty-fifth Sunday of the Year)

Jesus said to his disciples, "There was a rich man who had a steward, and charges were brought to him that this man was wasting his goods. And he called him and said to him, 'What is this that I hear about you? Turn in the account of your stewardship, for you can no longer be steward.'

"And the steward said to himself, 'What shall I do, since the master is taking the stewardship away from me? I am not strong enough to dig, and I am ashamed to beg. I have decided what to do, so that people may receive me into their houses when I am put out of the stewardship.' So, summoning his master's debtors one by one, he said to the first, 'How much do you owe my master?' He said, 'A hundred measures of oil.' And he said to him, 'Take your bill, and sit down quickly and write fifty.' Then he said to another, 'And how much do you owe?' He said, 'A hundred measures of wheat.' He said to him, 'Take your bill, and write eighty.' The master commended the dishonest steward for his prudence; for the sons of this world are wiser in their own generation than the children of light.

"And I tell you, make friends for yourselves by means of unrighteous mammon, so that when it fails they may receive you into the eternal habitations.

"He who is faithful in a very little is faithful also in much. If then you have not been faithful in the unrighteous mammon, who will entrust to you the true riches? And if you have not been faithful in that which is another's, who will give you that which is your own?

"No servant can serve two masters; for either he will hate the one and love the other, or he will be devoted to the one and despise the other. You cannot serve God and mammon."

(Luke 16:1-13)

***

When one speaks of wealth or, better, of money, one must not risk being misunderstood. We want to justify those little coins that pass from hand to hand among us; they may be many or few, but they are always somewhat shady and slippery; we don't know where they come from or where they'll end up.

Well (you'll say), they *do* come from our work, and we know quite well what our work is: honest, clean stuff that has never hurt anyone and has even helped some people, perhaps even society as a whole.

But do we really know fully how clean our work and therefore our money is, be it a little or a lot? For, I repeat, the Gospel doesn't say that only wealth, that is, an abundant amount of money, is condemnable.

Come now, let's be honest. When money is in question, the waters get muddied, as did the behavior of the cunning steward in the parable, one of those dishonest but charming types of which the world is full: so shrewd and unscrupulous that in the end he is praised by the very master he has defrauded.

And what on earth is meant by the enigmatic statement, "Make friends for yourselves by means of unrighteous mammon"? Does it mean that a legitimate and meritorious use of money is possible? Maybe so, but even when used well, riches are always called "dishonest." Therefore, in and of itself money is not saved. Even if we use it for charity, there is always something about it that a Christian does not want to have anything to do with and ought not have anything to do with.

But (we ask ourselves) what of our hard-earned pay envelopes and our little savings, aren't they innocent? I wouldn't say innocent; at most a necessary evil, but always an evil, a source of endless anxieties, apprehensiveness, discontent, quarrels, etc., etc.

No, let us regard as good advice what is said at the end of our Gospel passage, for here there is no possible mistake: "No servant can serve two masters": God and money.

I Love Myself Enough to Die

(Twenty-sixth Sunday of the Year)

"There was a rich man, who was clothed in purple and fine linen and who feasted sumptuously every day. And at his gate lay a poor man named Lazarus, full of sores, who desired to be fed from the rich man's table; moreover the dogs came and licked his sores.

"The poor man died and was carried off by the angels to Abraham's bosom. The rich man also died and was buried; and in Hades, being in torment, he lifted up his eyes, and saw Abraham afar off and Lazarus in his bosom. And he called out, 'Father Abraham, have mercy upon me, and send Lazarus to dip the end of his finger in water and cool my tongue; for I am in anguish in this flame.' But Abraham said, 'Son, remember that you in your lifetime received your good things, and Lazarus in like manner evil things; but now he is comforted here, and you are in anguish. And besides all this, between us and you a great chasm is fixed, in order that those who would pass from here to there may not be able, and none may cross from there to us.'

"And he said, 'Then I beg you, father, to send him to my father's house, for I have five brothers, so that he may warn them, lest they also come into this place of torment.' But Abraham said, 'They have Moses and the prophets; let them hear them.' And he said, 'No, father Abraham, but if some one goes to them from the dead, they will repent.' He said to him, 'If they do not hear Moses and the prophets, neither will they be convinced if some one should rise from the dead.' "

(Luke 16:19-31)

***

Once again the subject is money and riches: that stubborn, treacherous, insuperable obstacle that stands in the way of salvation wherever we turn. Today we have reached the "rich glutton." I remember hearing, when I was a child, of this poor unfortunate who ended up being roasted in hell, simply because he was rich and a glutton. As a result we took him, and still take him, lightly: What do we have in common with such a fellow? Do we dress in purple and fine linen and eat sumptuous feasts? Not at all! Who has any concern nowadays with all that stuff? The dress is passé. We eat a meager little steak and a not very flavorsome salad, and that's it; we have to get back to work, and besides, we have this damnable tendency to put on weight! Yes, we tend to put on weight, but it's certainly not from eating; it's the stress that does it.

As for the poor, what has happened to them? Who sees them any more? Perhaps it's because we're too busy; perhaps it's the stress, once again, that has caused the poor to disappear. In short, here we are, completely blind, blinded by our new and unequaled wealth: our very selves. Not by fine clothes or rich delicacies, not by vanity or gluttony, but by ourselves, only ourselves. We are tremendously focused on ourselves; our ego preoccupies us: If we eat little, we do so for its sake; if we toil with gritted teeth without looking to right or left, it is always for its sake; if we allow ourselves little presents, it is once again for its sake, not to create an appearance but to satisfy it. In short, we do everything in order that our ego may be happy. We love ourselves with all our heart. We are our own deities; there you see our entire wealth, and woe to anyone who touches it! And let not the dead or the prophets come and disturb us!

The Sycamores Hasten to the Sea

(Twenty-seventh Sunday of the Year)

The apostles said to the Lord, "Increase our faith!" And the Lord said, "If you had faith as a grain of mustard seed, you could say to this sycamore tree, 'Be rooted up, and be planted in the sea,' and it would obey you.

"Will any one of you, who has a servant plowing, or keeping sheep, say to him when he has come in from the field, 'Come at once and sit down at table'? Will he not rather say to him, 'Prepare supper for me, and gird yourself and serve me, till I eat and drink: and afterward you shall eat and drink'? Does he thank the servant because he did what was commanded? So you also, when you have done all that is commanded you, say, 'We are unworthy servants; we have only done what was our duty.'"

(Luke 17:5-10)

***

When all is said and done, what is a Christian? What are we who call ourselves Christians? Are we perhaps to be counted among the wretched underclass of people who are always somewhat downcast and are barely tolerated in an increasingly secularized world where they are treated as individuals with a handicap or a recurring immaturity, second-class individuals who lack sufficient confidence in themselves? In short, among the deluded, or even among the somewhat retarded?

Do not take offense, since this is, for the most part, the public image of a Christian. Moreover, the fault is our own and no one else's. That is always the case, for we believe and do not believe; we want but do not want sufficiently; we are afraid of being thought irrational, and so we trade in our faith for common sense; we confuse tolerance with an unconditional bowing to the opinions of the world, and we try to be like everyone else.

But Christians are not like everyone else. They believe firmly and literally that by the power of their faith they can uproot a sycamore tree and cause it to be transplanted in the sea. Yes, even though they no longer dare say so openly, Christians believe in miracles. And not only in the miracles of the saints, the miracles of past ages which are regarded as incidents in a nice edifying story, but in miracles that can happen at any moment, here and now, in my town, in my home. Christians believe firmly that if their faith is only as big as a mustard seed, they will be able to perform miracles.

This is our strength, this is what scandalizes others. Christians, then, are far from being a wretched folk who are backward in relation to the world! But we also know that whatever miracle of love and will we may have performed, we will have done no more than be consistent with our Christian name and our faith.

Everything Is Grace

(Twenty-eighth Sunday of the Year)

On the way to Jerusalem Jesus was passing along between Samaria and Galilee. And as he entered a village, he was met by ten lepers, who stood at a distance and lifted up their voices and said, "Jesus, Master, have mercy on us." When he saw them he said to them, "Go and show yourselves to the priests." And as they went they were cleansed. Then one of them, when he saw that he was healed, turned back, praising God with a loud voice; and he fell on his face at Jesus' feet, giving him thanks. Now he was a Samaritan. Then said Jesus, "Were not ten cleansed? Where are the nine? Was no one found to return and give praise to God except this foreigner?" And he said to him, "Rise and go your way. Your faith has made you well."

(Luke 17:11-19)

***

The tenth leper: I wonder what became of him after Jesus told him "Go"? Where did he go? How did he earn a living? Did he remember, the next day, a year later, that he had been healed by a miracle of God, or did his joy at recovering his bodily health make him forget that he was a living proof of the mercy and power of God, and did he say instead, "Enjoy, now that you can"? And how long did he enjoy? How long did his body remain healthy? How old was this leper? Was he already elderly, or was he young, with a whole life before him that would be stamped by the passage of God, who in the long run burns more deeply than leprosy? Did he feel this new burning, no longer in his body but in his spirit? Where was he when Jesus ascended the cross? Did he not listen further to Jesus? Did he follow him from a distance? What did he understand of Jesus?

We are not given answers to any of these questions. We know only that he was a foreigner, a Samaritan, and that at this moment in his life his faith made him well. But what did he believe in, more than the other nine did? They too obeyed and went to the priests as Jesus had commanded them; therefore they too believed that they could be healed. And in fact they were healed. But they did not come back to "give praise to God." Is it, then, so difficult to recognize a divine intervention in our lives? It seems that it is, since nine lepers out of ten received the favor with indifference, as something due to them.

There you have the mistake: to accept life without a sense of wonder; to mistake our poor presence on the face of the earth for the only event truly worth noting; no longer to be surprised; to be unable to see the hand of God in things both small and great; to look to the pages of the newspaper for the explanation of life; to be unable to see miracles.

The Beating of the Heart

(Twenty-ninth Sunday of the Year)

Jesus told his disciples a parable, to the effect that they ought always to pray and not lose heart. He said, "In a certain city there was a judge who neither feared God nor regarded man; and there was a widow in that city who kept coming to him and saying, 'Vindicate me against my adversary.' For a while he refused; but afterward he said to himself, 'Though I neither fear God nor regard man, yet because this widow bothers me, I will vindicate her, or she will wear me out by her continual coming.'" And the Lord said, "Hear what the unrighteous judge says. And will not God vindicate his elect, who cry to him day and night? Will he delay long over them? I tell you, he will vindicate them speedily. Nevertheless, when the Son of man comes, will he find faith on earth?"

(Luke 18:1-8)

***

But (you will say) it is easy to pray. Who does not pray when prayer becomes a felt need? All that is required is a general Catholic education, a remnant of faith, and let us admit it, a bit of superstition: Then, in a time of fear or anxiety or need, when our interests or our human affections urge us, there we are, praying away. Even the widow in the parable was under the pressure of her little business that had not been settled; besides, the poor thing had every reason to call for a justice that had never been done to her because she was a widow and therefore defenseless.

Well, that's how things go in this world, and that's how they go in the parable. I have never seen so many candles lit before statues of our Lady or special saints as in the period of school examinations. And why not? Isn't it permissible to call upon a friend, someone we believe able to help us in time of need? Isn't that the human way? And what are we if not human beings, that is, mixtures of weakness and strength, of shabbiness and greatness? So even the candles are quite in place.

But that is easy prayer, the kind that comes in spurts. There is also a continuous, unceasing prayer that does not ask for anything in particular because it asks for everything; the prayer whose rhythm the mystics compare with breathing or the beating of the heart. This is the prayer that transforms the world and turns life into a continual act of thanksgiving and faith, a continual plea for forgiveness because the world has need of forgiveness at every moment.

But prayer presupposes faith. It is impossible to pray if one does not have faith in the one being prayed to. When human beings are no longer able to pray, faith will have vanished from the earth.

Lament of an Old-Style Believer

(Thirtieth Sunday of the Year)

Jesus told this parable to some who trusted in themselves that they were righteous and despised others: "Two men went up into the temple to pray, one a Pharisee and the other a tax collector. The Pharisee stood and prayed thus with himself, 'God, I thank thee that I am not like other men, extortioners, unjust, adulterers, or even like this tax collector. I fast twice a week, I give tithes of all that I get.' But the tax collector, standing far off, would not even lift up his eyes to heaven, but beat his breast, saying, 'God, be merciful to me a sinner!' I tell you, this man went down to his house justified rather than the other, for every one who exalts himself will be humbled, but he who humbles himself will be exalted."

(Luke 18:9-14)

***

Don't take offense. It's clear that when I speak of "Christians" I'm referring to those average Christians whom we meet at Sunday Mass and then do not see again during the week; it's as though they had disappeared. Where do Christians go on weekdays? Who knows?

What concerns me, however, is this: How many of us Christians would be in a position, if it suited us, to offer at least the prayer of the Pharisee? Who of us can say in conscience that we have never cheated a neighbor of even a penny? That we have never done an injustice to those who live and work at our side? That we have never lusted after the wife or husband of another, even in the movies? That we have scrupulously observed the commandments of the Church and paid the taxes we owed?

When, then, we rebuke ourselves by saying, "Yes, I am just like the Pharisee of the parable," we are indulging in an act of pride. We are presupposing that we are already perfect enough to look down upon the undoubted good qualities of the Pharisee. And the best part is this: We are never so empty handed before God as when we stand there fearless and quite certain, I will not say of our merits (for we know we have none) but of a kind of credit in God's books, creatures standing straight up before their creator and telling him, "You're well aware, of course, that such is human nature and such the world in which we live. Where, then, is the sin? Everything is so justifiable that I am not even capable of sinning. For what, then, am I to ask forgiveness?" And we leave confession to the people with tender consciences, the irresolute, the "old-style believers."

Black Bread

(All Souls Day)

Jesus said to the crowds: "All that the Father gives me will come to me; and him who comes to me I will not cast out. For I have come down from heaven, not to do my own will, but the will of him who sent me, that I should lose nothing of all that he has given me, but raise it up at the last day. For this is the will of my Father, that every one who sees the Son and believes in him should have eternal life; and I will raise him up at the last day."

(John 6:37-40)

***

Therefore nothing will be lost; not even a crumb will be wasted. Our tired humanity, our weary bodies that are worn out by an unbroken, burdensome succession of little everyday actions, will not be cast aside at the hour of our death when it will seem that everything has been in vain: goodness, patience, honesty, suffering, devotion. Death, the enemy that entered human history through the fissure made by sin, seems to toss everything onto a heap in which nothing can be distinguished; it seems to deride and render useless the daily efforts of human beings and to annihilate even the most modest hope.

If death were truly to conquer and sweep everything away, as a drunkard falls from his chair and drags the sumptuously laden tablecloth with him to the floor, then our actions would indeed be meaningless. I am referring especially to those little actions, unknown to anyone except the person and God, that form the real fabric of social and civic life but earn no reward and have no merit in the world's eyes: the crumbs, the fine dust, the Milky Way, of history. They form the great nebula of the "common man," that is, those who will never get themselves talked about in the newspapers or on television and will never even see their names mentioned in the most modest category of service.

Even these people, whose picture, "portrait of an unknown person," resembles each of us will be sought out and raised up to an everlasting life, alongside the highest dignitaries and the rulers of the world. I like to imagine that on that last day even the smallest crumb of black bread will be gathered up while whole cakes will be thrown into the trash. Death is overcome and with death injustice, malfeasance, and violence. But on one condition: that everything in our lives has been done for love of Christ.

Eternity Between Four Walls

(Dedication of St. John Lateran)

The [Samaritan] woman said to Jesus, "Sir, I perceive that you are a prophet. Our fathers worshiped on this mountain; and you say that in Jerusalem is the place where men ought to worship." Jesus said to her, "Woman, believe me, the hour is coming when neither on this mountain nor in Jerusalem will you worship the Father. You worship what you do not know; we worship what we know, for salvation is from the Jews. But the hour is coming, and now is, when the true worshipers will worship the Father in spirit and truth, for such the Father seeks to worship him. God is spirit, and those who worship him must worship in spirit and truth."

(John 4:19-24)

***

The subject once again is prayer, but this time in its most intense and unqualified form: adoration. Human beings come before God and acknowledge that they are his creatures; they turn to him as to their supreme good, their reason for living. Do we not say, for example, that we adore someone when that person's existence is more necessary to us than the air we breathe and when our every action and desire is focused on that person?

If this be the case, then it is clear to us that the walls within which this act of unqualified love takes place are unimportant, that the dignity of the place where the act occurs is irrelevant. I knew a man who admitted that for a lengthy period in his life he locked himself in the bathroom for a few minutes when he wanted to pray to God. He was certainly not a mystic; in fact, he was so completely caught up in concrete everyday tasks that he never had a minute for himself; his house was so crowded that he did not have even a small area to himself. In the evening, however (but not even every evening was this possible), when he felt himself going to pieces and experienced a vast desire to pull himself together in God's presence, he would lock himself up in the only place available; there he would kneel on the floor and rest his joined hands on the rim of the bathtub. This cubbyhole became his temple, the place where he offered adoration.

It sounds like something out of Dostoyevski, but not even Dostoyevski ever invented anything so true to life. The man told me his story in all simplicity, laughing a bit at himself.

One morning, I saw God being adored beside a pillar in the Central Station of Milan: It was a woman, and she was kneeling on the floor. "Obviously unbalanced!" Really? Let the worshipers of rationality make such a claim; a Christian cannot make it.

Bent over a Plate of Soup

(Thirty-third Sunday of the Year)

As some spoke of the temple, how it was adorned with noble stones and offerings, he said, "As for these things which you see, the days will come when there shall not be left here one stone upon another that will not be thrown down." And they asked him, "Teacher, when will this be, and what will be the sign when this is about to take place?"

And he said, "Take heed that you are not led astray; for many will come in my name, saying, 'I am he!' and 'The time is at hand!' Do not go after them. And when you hear of wars and tumults, do not be terrified; for this must first take place, but the end will not be at once."

Then he said to them, "Nation will rise against nation, and kingdom against kingdom; there will be great earthquakes, and in various places famines and pestilences; and there will be terrors and great signs from heaven. But before all this they will lay their hands on you and persecute you, delivering you up to the synagogues and prisons, and you will be brought before kings and governors for my name's sake. This will be a time for you to bear testimony. Settle it therefore in your minds, not to meditate beforehand how to answer; for I will give you a mouth and wisdom, which none of your adversaries will be able to withstand or contradict. You will be delivered up even by parents and brothers and kinsmen and friends, and some of you they will put to death; you will be hated by all for my name's sake. But not a hair of your head will perish. By your endurance you will gain your lives."

(Luke 21:5-19)

***

As we take our ease in our homes, sitting unconcerned in front of our television sets, perhaps resting in an armchair or with our supper in front of us, we watch images of blood and death pass before our eyes, beamed in from all parts of a world that is becoming ever smaller, ever closer and more violent. We see Christ's prophecies being fulfilled, but nothing changes in our lives. It is as if this passage of the Gospel and even these images had no power to unsettle us; we pretend that they are not part of our present life.

Our sickness consists in our being incapable of attention; in deluding ourselves that the terror and violence are just elements of a nasty film, a film about a nightmare that visits us daily and which we resist by means of our little self-centeredness, our deafness and apathy, that is, our inability to suffer with others and to acknowledge that no one is saved in isolation. After centuries of wars, carnage, and revolutions we no longer believe in the return of Christ or even in the coming of new prophets. Humanity has grown weary of expecting salvation from human beings, but it has also grown weary of expecting it from Christ. We no longer believe in anything or anyone, no sign is enough for us, no calamity moves us, no miracle convinces us. Nothing has value any longer, everything is bankrupt, it's every man for himself, even God is not accepted by all; rather each individual adores his or her own very personal god, of which they never dare speak. Who, then, could ever be in a position to persecute us?

Christians, we have turned our faith into something private. We are so tolerant that we smile when someone publicly expresses contempt for what we silently believe in. Prophecies are not for us; in the presence of signs from heaven we turn away. Our lives have become tedious; we suffer but no longer know why. We are no longer of any use either to Christ or to Antichrist.

Today You Will Be with Me

(Christ the King)

The people stood by, watching; but the rulers scoffed at him, saying, "He saved others; let him save himself, if he is the Christ of God, his Chosen One!" The soldiers also mocked him, coming up and offering him vinegar, and saying, "If you are the King of the Jews, save yourself!" There was also an inscription over him, "This is the King of the Jews."

One of the criminals who were hanged railed at him, "Are you not the Christ? Save yourself and us!" But the other rebuked him, saying, "Do you not fear God, since you are under the same sentence of condemnation? And we indeed justly; for we are receiving the due reward of our deeds; but this man has done nothing wrong." And he said, "Jesus, remember me when you come in your kingly power." And he said to him, "Truly, I say to you, today you will be with me in Paradise."

(Luke 23:35-43)

***

Here, at last, beyond the sufferings, the doubts, and the anxieties and regardless of our unworthiness, the words of truthful promise reach us; here Christ extends his brotherly hand, as if he had unnailed it from the cross and extended it to us across space and time in order to draw us to himself and bestow his glory and peace upon us: "Today you will be with me in Paradise."

The words are the words of a king, but a king who suffers with us and for us. The promise is that his kingdom is already here at hand. Right now: this very day. Every day we find ourselves unworthy of belonging to that kingdom; but every day, too, forgiveness and the promise reach us from the cross. Let no one be discouraged by his or her life; let no one be scandalized. Life, no matter how it has been lived, is a priceless possession because it is our only means of encountering Christ. No existence ever deserves contempt because every life contains—perhaps still hidden, perhaps still distant—a moment of salvation, the moment in which, even while absorbed by our worries and nailed to our own crosses, we lift up our eyes and discover the cross of Christ standing there alongside our own.

This is the paradox in which we live daily: Though we have no merits and our poor hands are empty and our days are so short and profitless, we are nonetheless heirs of a kingdom. "Jesus, remember me," now, this very moment, while I am still a pilgrim in the world, while I am still breathlessly involved in my insignificant "important" human affairs. "Remember me" at every moment of my day. And let the reign of God come and fill up the emptiness of our lives.